THE WISCONSIN CAPITOL

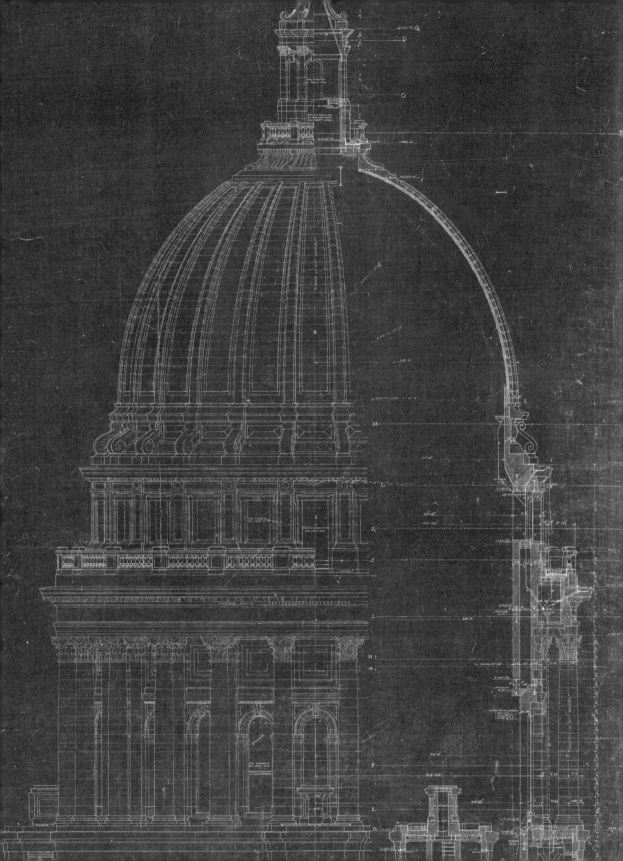

CONTENTS

PREFACE

AN EXPERIMENT IN DEMOCRACY

When Europeans first settled here, Wisconsin was ruled by a king.

King Louis XIV governed all of Canada, including "Ouisconsin," from 1661 to 1715. In June 1671, his emissary planted a cross beside Lake Superior and announced that the whole region was part of France, an astounding act of arrogance. But it didn't astound the explorers and missionaries who witnessed it. They believed that God gave kings the power to rule over everyone else. This divine right of kings was common sense for centuries.

That is, it was common sense until a handful of visionaries in Philadelphia hatched a crazy idea in 1776. "We hold these truths to be self-evident," their theory ran, "that all men are created equal, that they are endowed by their Creator with certain unalienable Rights, that among these are Life, Liberty and the pursuit of Happiness.—That to secure these rights, Governments are instituted among Men, deriving their just powers from the consent of the governed . . ."

The Founding Fathers turned the world upside down by proclaiming that political power doesn't descend from God on high, but rises up from the hearts and minds of the people.

Wisconsin pioneers tested this theory between 1830 and 1860. Thousands of dreamers and schemers left East Coast cities, Southern plantations, British fiefdoms, and German principalities to try their hands at self-governance in the wilderness. They held

Opposite: Capitol dome photographed by James T. Potter

meetings, chose their neighbors to be lawmakers, and sent those neighbors to Madison to realize the Founding Fathers' dream of freedom and democracy.

Reality, unfortunately, didn't quite live up to the dream. Wisconsin's 1848 constitution excluded over half of the state's population from participating in democracy; women, African Americans, and Native Americans were all denied the right to vote. Candidates for office were soon being chosen by party bosses who drew up the ballots behind closed doors. Government jobs were handed out in exchange for votes or campaign donations. By the mid-nineteenth century, the ideal of democracy had evolved into rich white men trading favors in smoke-filled backrooms.

But the Founding Fathers' vision survived. The idea of self-government took root and, like a flower rising from a crack in the sidewalk, democracy slowly but surely began to flourish in Wisconsin. In 1866, African American men secured the vote. In 1884, women won partial suffrage. In 1895, a civil rights bill passed. In 1899, the worst electoral bribery was outlawed. In 1904, primary elections replaced secret deals among the rich and powerful.

Then, the Wisconsin Capitol burned to the ground.

That's right. Just as the doors to democracy were opening wider than ever before, our most visible symbol of self-rule went up in flames.

The state's leaders vowed to create a new capitol to embody their dream of democracy. They spared no expense as architects, designers, painters, sculptors, and craftsmen worked on the building for more than a decade. When the Capitol we know today was finished in 1917, it was part office block, part museum, and part shrine.

As the decades passed, everyone found room under its generous dome—Yankee and German, Norwegian and Ho-Chunk, women and men, Republican and Democrat, black and white, gay and straight, progressive and conservative. This book recounts some of their stories and pays homage to Wisconsin's grand monument to freedom and democracy.

1

In the Beginning

In 1837, when workers began building Madison's first capitol, people had been living on the isthmus for more than ten thousand years. At the end of the last Ice Age, melting glaciers flooded hundreds of square miles in what is now central Dane County. Rising out of this Glacial Lake Yahara was the rounded hilltop where today's state capitol stands. Small bands of hunters speared mammals, caught fish, and gathered plants all around the water's edge for thousands of years, and the remains of their keyhole-shaped cellars and stone tools can be found in abundance around the Madison region. Around 500 BCE, native peoples began burying their deceased leaders in conical or linear-shaped mounds, which can still be seen around the city.

In approximately 800 CE, residents of what would become Madison started sculpting mounds into the shapes of eagles, geese, bears, deer, snakes, and mythical creatures. More than six hundred of these effigy mounds once ringed the city's four lakes. The site of the modern capitol contained several of these

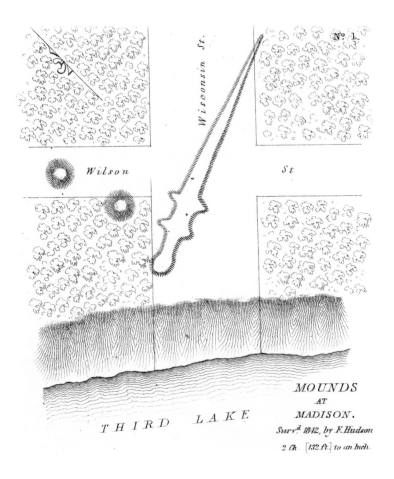

mounds, including a dramatic "water panther" longer than a football field that overlooked Lake Monona from the corner of today's West Wilson Street and Martin Luther King Drive. Archaeologist Bob Birmingham concluded that "one could rightly consider Lake Mendota the symbolic capital of the whole effigy mound region" that stretched from the shores of Lake Michigan across the Mississippi River into Iowa. Today's Capitol Square was hallowed ground for at least a thousand years before white people arrived.

Archaeologists generally agree the effigy mound builders were probably ancestors of the Ho-Chunk Indians. In 1829, a census by a US Indian agent counted nearly six hundred Ho-Chunk residents living around the Madison lakes. One Ho-Chunk village was located just north of today's capitol, where a steep ridge protected it from winter winds; south-facing slopes supported the growth of corn, beans, and squash; and the lake at the foot of the hill made for easy fishing. This sunny slope was home to sacred effigy mounds for a thousand years, until nineteenth-century white settlers constructed streets and houses on Mansion Hill.

When the first government surveyor, John Mullett, arrived on Madison's isthmus in 1834, he found a few hundred Ho-Chunk families and a fur trader named Oliver Armel living just north of today's capitol. Armel had settled with the Ho-Chunk in about 1821 and helped keep them from siding with the Sauk during the 1832 Black Hawk War. When the war ended, he set up a trading post just north of the current capitol, where he exchanged manufactured goods and liquor for furs. When federal troops forced the Ho-Chunk out of Wisconsin in the 1840s, Armel went with them. He died on their Nebraska reservation sometime after 1870.

Until the summer of 1836, none of this mound-building, exploring, fighting, fur-trading, and surveying had happened in Wisconsin, technically speaking, because there was no legal entity with that name. The area had, at various times, been part of the Spanish (1512–1627), French (1628–1762), and British (1762–1783) empires before the United States took control in 1783. Soon after, it became part of Michigan Territory, which stretched westward from Detroit all the way to the Great Plains.

When Michigan became a state in 1836, the land west of Lake Michigan was formed into a new Wisconsin Territory, spreading from Green Bay across modern Iowa, Minnesota, and half of the Dakotas. Congress enacted a law establishing it on April 20, 1836, and on July 4 of that year, Henry Dodge took office as its first governor.

In 1827, Dodge brought slaves with him from the South to open lead mines on land illegally seized from the Ho-Chunk. In 1832, when Sauk Indians tried to reoccupy their homeland, he commanded local militia in the Black Hawk War, which culminated in

Undated portrait of
Governor Henry Dodge

WHI IMAGE ID 2613

Doty's plat of
Madison, 1836

the ruthless slaughter of hundreds of women and children at the Battle of Bad Axe.

In 1836, Dodge decided to let the voters choose their own capital, which was the most important question debated at the territorial convention that fall. Milwaukee was just a fur trading post with a single house, so that city didn't seem a likely choice. Residents of Green Bay, the oldest town in Wisconsin, wanted the honor, but most of the population actually lived in the lead mining region southwest of modern Dodgeville. And residents of what is now Iowa thought the capital should be centrally located somewhere on the Mississippi River.

The territorial convention met from October 25 to December 9, 1836, at Belmont, in the lead mining region. Wisconsin's first lawmakers at this gathering were far from expert statesmen. "I find as I anticipated," Green Bay delegate Henry Baird wrote home to his wife, "a great want of legal talent. . . . The representation is, however, for a new country, by no means despicable, and much superior to my expectations." Delegates deliberated and slept in two hastily assembled wooden buildings that were drafty and inhospitable for the cold autumn days.

The agenda initially focused on more mundane matters, but perpetual side conversations revolved around which location would be named the territorial capital. "Numerous speculators were in attendance," one of the attendees recalled, "with beautiful maps of prospective cities, whose future greatness was portrayed with all the fervor and eloquence which the excited imagination of their proprietors could display."

When the capital question finally came up for debate, arguments raged for two days. James Doty, the only delegate who'd actually seen most of the proposed locations, wanted none of them. Instead, he proposed that the territorial capital should be set on an obscure isthmus in the Four Lakes region that he'd visited on his way to the convention—and, conveniently, where he and a couple of friends had just bought all the best real estate. He called it Madison in honor of Founding Father James Madison, who had recently died.

On November 23, a draft bill naming this isthmus the seat of government was introduced. "A spirited attack was made upon it," one member wrote, "and motions to strike out Madison and insert some other place were successively made in favor of Fond du Lac, Dubuque, Portage, Helena, Milwaukee, Racine, Belmont, Mineral Point, Platteville, Green Bay, Cassville, Belleview, Koshkonong, Wisconsinapolis, Peru, and Wisconsin City." Each of those motions failed to win a majority.

By then, winter was setting in and the delegates were sleeping on bare wooden floors in the frigid building. "Doty supplied himself with a full stock of buffalo robes," an eyewitness remembered, "and went around camping with the members, and making them as comfortable as he could," while also trying to win their votes. He unrolled a hand-drawn map showing the isthmus divided into streets and blocks, and held private conversations during which "Madison town lots in large numbers were freely distributed among members, their friends, and others who were supposed to possess influence with them." By the time the final vote was called, sixteen of the thirty-nine delegates, the clerks of both houses, and Governor Dodge's son all owned new property on Madison's isthmus.

On November 28, 1836, the bill naming Madison as Wisconsin's capital finally passed, and lawmakers rushed home to their fireplaces. The humble wood-frame building in Belmont where Wisconsin's government was born was sold to a farmer who used it as a stable. Meanwhile, as settlers flocked to Madison over the next several years, Doty and his partners made $35,510 on their initial real estate investment of $2,400, and Doty was appointed the second territorial governor by the new president, John Tyler, in 1841.

Roseline and Eben Peck left Blue Mounds for Madison in the spring of 1837 to construct an inn that would house the workers needed to erect the state capitol. She was the city's first white female resident, and her memoirs highlight details of that time that male authors left out. "Pshaw," she protested in response to the men's accounts, "talk about the time that tried men's soul, just as if a woman had none."

Peck reached Madison while seven months pregnant, with a young son and an unreliable husband, at the same moment that a vicious spring blizzard descended on the capital. "Well now, here we are at Madison on the 15th [of April, 1837]," she wrote afterward, "sitting in a wagon under a tree with a bed-quilt thrown over my own and little boy's heads in a tremendous storm of snow and sleet, twenty-five miles from any inhabitants on one side [Blue Mounds] and nearly one hundred on the other [Milwaukee]."

"We were well aware what our business would be when settled," she wrote, and so "we provided ourselves accordingly, and purchased at Mineral Point over one hundred dollars worth of groceries, as I have the bills now to show." Her first guests arrived two weeks later, and though Peck had no beds for them, she

Portrait of Roseline Peck in 1874

WHI IMAGE ID 3941

THE WISCONSIN CAPITOL

wrote, "Well, we had a spacious dining-room—under the broad canopy of heaven." The Peck cabin was located roughly where today's Butler Street meets East Wilson Street, just behind the modern state office buildings above the north shore of Lake Monona. Soon, according to surveyor Franklin Hatheway, two other primitive hotels sprang up, including "a large one-and-a-half story frame boarding house and tavern, the entire upper floor being one bare room with rows of beds on each side under the eaves and a passage-way through the middle barely high enough to allow a man to stand erect."

Doty told Peck, "Madam, prepare yourself for company on the Fourth [of July, 1837], as a large number from Milwaukee, Mineral Point, Fort Winnebago, and Galena have concluded to meet here for the purpose of viewing the place and celebrating the day. . . . Just constitute me your agent, and I will contract for whatever you want." She told Doty to order lumber from the Wisconsin River and dishes, fixtures, provisions, wines, food, and bedding from Mineral Point. A herd of Illinois cattle that was being driven to Green Bay serendipitously appeared on July 2, providing meat for the festivities.

On the evening of July 3, the lumber arrived, and by one o'clock the next day, the dining room floor was laid, a table built, and the holiday dinner cooked. Her guests included Doty, his friend Morgan Martin, thirty-six workmen who came to build the Capitol, and a large assembly of Ho-Chunk Indians with their chief Mau-nah-pay-ho-nik, known to the whites as Dandy. "In the evening there was a basket of champagne carried into the dining-room," she recalled, "and . . . good feeling, friendship, and hilarity prevailed generally." The Capitol's ceremonial cornerstone was laid, and the festivities continued for as long as the food and liquor held out—three full days.

Roseline and Eben Peck's cabin, the first house in Madison, was built in 1837.

2

EARLY CAPITOLS

The contract for building a capitol in Madison was awarded to Augustus Bird of Milwaukee. He left that city on foot on May 26, 1837, with thirty-six carpenters and laborers, six yoke of oxen, wagons, tools, cooking utensils, and other supplies. They arrived on the isthmus on June 10 after a two-week hike through forests, over prairies, and across wetlands, mostly in a steady rain. The construction workers were paid $2.25 per day. They quickly built a dormitory for themselves beside Lake Monona, where the mosquitoes were so thick at night that they kept a fire burning on the floor to smoke them out. New workers kept drifting in, and by the end of the summer, Bird's crew numbered nearly one hundred.

Conditions were primitive, progress was slow, materials were crude, and much of the work on the Capitol was improvised. The men quarried stone for the foundation and walls at Maple Bluff on the other side of Lake Mendota, paddled it to the isthmus in scows, and then dragged it up the hill. Ancient trees around the building site were felled for lumber and cut into beams and planks using a steam sawmill. At one point, workers went on strike because the paper money they received as wages turned out to be worth less than face value when they tried to deposit it in a bank.

Their progress, one worker noted, was regularly delayed by a "half-breed Frenchman, living with some Indians in the adjoining woods, who had a natural propensity to possess himself of valuable articles, such as axes, hand-saws, hammers, hatchets, shovels, etc., almost any article for which we had daily use. He often came to know if we had lost anything, and, if we had, would at once commence negotiations for the missing article. His terms were from one-half to two-thirds of its value. When the contract was concluded to his satisfaction, he would immediately go to camp and return with it, stating that some bad Indian had stolen it." The identity of the Frenchman remains a mystery.

Bird's instructions called for a two-story building, 104 feet by 54 feet, with a stone foundation and walls two feet thick above a shallow basement. Two 30-by-12-foot oak porches with four Doric columns graced the front and back sides, and the roof sported a 26-foot tin-covered dome in its center. Inside, the ground floor held a "great hall" under the dome, a circular room for the Territorial Council (equivalent to today's state senate) on one end, and a 40-foot-square House chamber on the other. Staircases carried spectators up to observation galleries and offices on the second floor.

However, a building of this magnitude could not be erected in a single summer. By November 1837, Bird had only finished laying the foundation when the workers all went home for the winter. The next spring, a new contract was awarded not to Bird but to Doty's friend James Morrison, who promised to have at least four walls, a roof, and the first-floor chambers ready for use by October 15, 1838. When lawmakers arrived in November of that year, however, they found wet plaster, ice-covered floorboards, and unfurnished halls without desks or benches.

"The floors were laid with green oak boards full of ice," one of them recalled, and once wood stoves had warmed up the floor, the

planks shrunk so much "that a person could run his hands between the boards." Breezes blew up from the exposed basement making the room so cold that lawmakers had to adjourn temporarily because their ink froze. To make matters worse, gaps in the foundation had enabled a herd of local pigs to occupy the basement.

Ebenezer Childs, a legislator from Green Bay, later admitted that when one of his colleagues droned on too long in those days, "I would take a long pole, go at the hogs, and stir them up; when they would raise a young pandemonium for noise and confusion, the speaker's voice would become completely drowned, and he would be compelled to stop, not, however, without giving his squealing disturbers a sample of his swearing ability." Pigs lived under the legislature for another decade, putting a new spin on the notion of "pork" in state government (never mind the odors that must have permeated the halls of justice).

In addition to pranks like Childs's, visiting lawmakers also indulged in bad behavior. "When the Legislature assembled," recalled Madison's first historian, Daniel Durrie, "it seemed to call together the worst elements of society. Faro banks [dens for playing card games of chance], a thing called 'The Tiger,' and other gambling institutions were said to exist, and to be run with great boldness." The Tiger was a two-story gambling den and bar on Pinckney Street erected in 1838. "Bad whisky, in large quantities, was said to be consumed," wrote Durrie, "much to the damage of the consumer."

When they weren't drinking or gambling, territorial legislators spent much of their time doling out public funds for "internal improvements" that profited themselves and their acquaintances. They were so corrupt that they earned the nickname "The Forty Thieves." Perhaps their lowest point came on February 11, 1842, when one legislator gunned down another on the floor of the legislature.

During a debate about a political appointment in the Territorial Council, Charles Arndt of Green Bay implied that fellow member James Vineyard had lied about the proposed candidate. Vineyard responded so angrily that the session was quickly adjourned. During the break, Arndt approached Vineyard's desk and demanded that he take back his accusations. When Vineyard refused, Arndt raised his hand and struck him in the head.

Before anyone could stop him, Vineyard took a step back, pulled out his pistol, and shot Arndt in the chest. Arndt fell to

This depiction of the shooting of Charles Arndt by James Vineyard was created by the staff artist for the *Milwaukee Journal* on April 30, 1953.

WHI IMAGE ID 23613

the floor and died about five minutes later. His father, visiting from Green Bay and observing the session from the newly completed spectators' gallery, watched his son die in a pool of blood on the floor of the legislature. English novelist Charles Dickens described the incident in his 1842 book, *American Notes*, citing it as an example of the "revolting evidences of the state of society" in the United States.

The earliest men who occupied the executive office in the ramshackle capitol were just as colorful as the legislators. After Henry Dodge, Madison promoter James Doty became the territory's second governor and insisted on using the idiosyncratic spelling "Wiskonsan." Territorial lawmakers refused to comply, since the federal law established the territory as "Wisconsin," and the dispute threatened to bring the entire government to a stalemate.

"Governor Doty and the legislature were in constant hostility," recalled pioneer settler Theodore Rodolf. "The governor had a fondness for spelling the name of the territory as 'Wiskonsan.' The legislature, in order to avoid future embarrassments and misunderstanding, found itself obliged to declare by a joint resolution that the spelling used in the organic act should be maintained." Doty eventually backed down, the government moved on to other business, and Doty later had no problem serving in Washington as a congressman from "Wisconsin."

Another notable early governor was Nathaniel Tallmadge, who was appointed in June 1844 just after a psychic premonition saved his life and turned him into a dedicated spiritualist. While visiting a warship on the Potomac, Tallmadge felt an irresistible urge to run away from the demonstration of a large cannon, which exploded seconds after he left. "I rushed on deck," he wrote, "saw the lifeless and mangled bodies, and found that the gun had burst at the very spot where I had stood." Shaken to the core, he began to attend séances, meet mediums, communicate with the dead, and write about his ghostly encounters.

Tallmadge claimed to receive messages from disembodied souls, including his deceased US Senate colleague John C. Calhoun.

Portrait of
Governor Nathaniel
Tallmadge, 1833

WHI IMAGE ID 2963

By tapping out letters on the dining room table, the ghost of Calhoun apparently explained that Tallmadge was seeing ghosts in order to "draw mankind together in harmony, and convince skeptics of the immortality of the soul." With the change of national administration in 1845, Tallmadge retired to his farm near Fond du Lac, where he practiced law while writing about spiritualism.

When Tallmadge left the Capitol in 1845, Henry Dodge was reappointed governor and charged with forcing the Ho-Chunk out of Wisconsin. After witnessing the slaughter of the Sauk at the Battle of Bad Axe, the Ho-Chunk had signed a treaty requiring them to move across the Mississippi River to the Turkey River in Iowa. But many of them refused to go, preferring to live as fugitives in the land of their ancestors.

Among the resistors was Chief Mau-nah-pay-ho-nik, or Dandy, who had attended Madison's first Fourth of July celebration at the Peck cabin in 1837. Troops caught up with him near Baraboo, shackled him in chains, and brought him before Governor Dodge. "Dandy produced a Bible from his bosom," recalled an eyewitness, "and asked the governor if it was a good book. Greatly surprised, the governor answered that it was. 'Then,' said Dandy, 'if a man could do all that was in that book, could any more be required of him?' Receiving a negative answer, he continued: 'Well, look that book all through, and if you find in it that Dandy ought to be removed by the government to Turkey River, I will go; but if you do not find it, I will stay here.'" Dodge was not amused and ordered Mau-nah-pay-ho-nik brought in chains to Fort Crawford at Prairie du Chien for deportation.

The chains blistered his legs so badly that Mau-nah-pay-ho-nik claimed he was unable to walk, so he was carried around the fort. After three weeks, it was decided that he should be taken across the river to Iowa. The guard, believing Mau-nah-pay-ho-nik couldn't walk, carried him to a buggy, removed the shackles, and went to get a whip. But as soon as the soldier's back was turned, the chief leaped out and disappeared up the Mississippi bluffs. Mau-nah-pay-ho-nik never did move west, but lived on the run for the rest of his life in western Wisconsin, helping his people evade detection and providing food and comfort to the needy.

Meanwhile, the partially constructed Capitol building where Governor Dodge worked continued to be plagued by problems. In 1839, after two years of construction, an investigating committee found that contractors "had done little more than erect a shell of a capitol, which is scarcely capable of sustaining its own weight, and which, unless it is speedily secured by extensive repairs, must become a heap of ruins." Work dragged on for another five years amid missed deadlines, shady deals, unpaid bills, lawsuits and countersuits, and regular threats from lawmakers who wanted to abandon the whole thing and move the capital to Milwaukee.

Carte-de-visite studio portrait of Mau-nah-pay-ho-nik, or Chief Dandy, ca. 1866

WHI IMAGE ID 61426

In 1842, Elizabeth Baird, wife of Green Bay legislator Henry Baird, visited Madison while the Capitol was under construction. She described it as "squatty-looking" and, noting the tin dome, suggested that the building should be called "Doty's Washbowl." The name caught on, maybe because, as legislator Moses M. Strong noted, the dome leaked "very badly and the rains were seriously injuring the interior of the building." Finally, in 1844, the original contractor, Augustus Bird, fixed the roof, completed the interior, and finished the rear porch.

Throughout the 1840s, white settlers continued to flood into Wisconsin Territory, and the population expanded from eleven thousand people in 1836 to more than three hundred thousand a decade later. This was enough for Wisconsin to qualify as a state, so in the fall of 1846 voters sent 124 representatives to Madison to draft a constitution. They met at the Capitol and argued for ten weeks before finally agreeing on a draft in December. Two of its provisions were unusual for their time.

Article XIV read, "On the Rights of Married Women . . . All property, real and personal, of the wife . . . shall be her separate property." These seemingly innocuous words sparked passionate debate among the delegates and in the media. In most states at the time, a wife's wages, inheritance, and other assets belonged to her husband or nearest male relative, and women could not

CONSTITUTION

OF THE

STATE OF WISCONSIN.

PREAMBLE.

THE constitution of the state of Wisconsin adopted in convention at Madison on the sixteenth day of December, in the year of our Lord One thousand eight hundred and forty six, and of the Independence of the United States, the seventy first.

We the people of Wisconsin, acknowledging, with gratitude, the grace and benificence of God, in permitting us to make choice of our form of Government, having the right of admission into the Union, as a member of the confederacy, consistent with the Constitution of the United States; and the ordinance of Congress of seventeen hundred and eighty seven, believing that the time had arrived when our present political condition ought to cease, and the right of self-government to be asserted; and in order to establish justice, promote the general welfare and secure the blessings of liberty, to ourselves and our posterity, do mutually agree with each other, to form ourselves into a free and independent State, by the name of "The State of Wisconsin", and do ordain and establish this constitution for the government thereof.

own property. But some forward-thinking Wisconsin utopians thought that women should be able to keep their earnings and assets. Opposing this group were critics who argued that women's property rights contradicted the Bible and would undermine the institution of marriage. All through the winter and spring of 1846 and 1847 the two sides argued over women's rights.

The second unusual thing about the proposed 1846 constitution was that it made banks illegal. Article X read, "The legislature shall not have power to authorize or incorporate, by any general or special law, any bank or other institution having any banking power or privilege." Delegates included this provision because, according to early settler Theodore Rodolf, in 1836 Wisconsin had been "flooded with a paper currency called 'shinplasters,' 'wild cats' and 'yellow dogs' which were based on cheek and had no capital to back them." When the federal government decided to accept only gold or silver as payment for land, banks across the nation folded and Wisconsin's financial infrastructure collapsed like a house of cards. Ten years later, framers of the 1846 constitution remembered those hard times and decided to outlaw privately owned banks.

In April 1847, the draft constitution went before the voters—all of them white males, by definition—and was emphatically rejected. A new constitutional convention went back to the drawing board and toned down or deleted the controversial articles. Their second draft made no mention of such alarming ideas as women's property rights. This version passed easily, and Wisconsin became the thirtieth US state in 1848.

The first order of business for the new state was to elect a governor. The dark horse who eventually won, Nelson Dewey, became another of our state's eccentric chief executives. Famous for chain-smoking cheap cigars and, as historian Victor Kutchin noted, "calling the average grafter 'a damned scoundrel,'" Dewey's most lasting legacy is our state motto, "Forward." He needed an official seal with which to emboss the new state's legal documents and asked University of Wisconsin chancellor John Lathrop to design one. Lathrop delivered a sketch inspired by European heraldry that repeated Wisconsin Territory's Latin motto, "Civilitas Successit Barbaruin" ("Civilization Succeeds Barbarism"). Dewey took it to New York to be cast in metal.

While there, he ran into Milwaukee attorney Edward Ryan. Neither of them liked Lathrop's fancy design with its pretentious Latin maxim, so they sat down on the steps of a Wall Street bank and started over from scratch. Ryan suggested that Wisconsin's state seal should repeat New York's motto, "Excelsior," but Dewey, who Kutchin later remembered as "not being an easy man

Undated portrait of Governor Nelson Dewey

WHI IMAGE ID 2407

to get along with [and] bound to have his way," didn't like it. Sitting on the stoop while pedestrians and horses passed by, they toyed with "Upward" and "Onward" before finally settling on "Forward." They also inserted a badger onto the seal as one of the new state's symbols. Their impromptu design, slightly tweaked, has survived for 150 years.

Being Wisconsin's first governor didn't guarantee Dewey fame or fortune, though. A staunch Democrat, he was marginalized when Republicans took control of the Capitol after the Civil War and Wisconsin became a one-party state. He eked out a living as a pugnacious attorney, but ultimately lost his savings, his home, and even his family to the proverbial slings and arrows of outrageous fortune. In old age, Dewey was given a sinecure as state prison inspector, living out of a suitcase and sleeping on a cot at Waupun. He died in 1889, wretchedly poor, and a friend speculated that most people "did not know whether he were living or dead."

Dewey was probably too honest to succeed on Wisconsin's morally ambiguous frontier. Historian Fred Holmes summarized life at the Capitol before the Civil War this way: "The political atmosphere was white-hot with partisanship; officials 'feathered their nests' at public expense; the vast land heritage of the state was wantonly squandered and the public morals touched bottom. It was an epoch fogged with political trickery and legislative chicanery." The depth of this corruption and deceit is epitomized by the gubernatorial election of 1855 and its aftermath.

Incumbent Democrat William Barstow assumed, as many Wisconsin residents did, that he was a shoe-in for re-election. His only challenger was an unknown candidate from a fledgling new party whose members called themselves "Republicans." As voters went to the polls, most people expected another easy Democratic victory. But when the dust settled, Barstow had won by just 157 votes, and his upstart Republican challenger, suspecting fraud, immediately demanded a recount.

The investigation was still in progress when inauguration day arrived on January 7, 1856, and both candidates claimed

Opposite: This state seal is painted on the ceiling of the Capitol's first floor corridor, off of the rotunda running toward West Washington Avenue.

WHI IMAGE ID 45095

Opposite: This 1855 map of Madison shows the development of the isthmus and the small size of the Capitol in comparison to the Capitol Square.

WHI IMAGE ID 23644

the governorship in separate ceremonies. Shortly afterward, the supreme court found that the Democrats had indeed rigged the election. Some votes reported as coming from outlying counties had been written on stationery used only inside the Capitol, and others had been counted from far northern townships where no voters actually lived.

Barstow resigned in humiliation on March 21, 1856, leaving his lieutenant governor, Arthur McArthur, in charge of the Capitol. Four days later, the supreme court named Republican Coles Bashford the winner, making McArthur's tenure of four days the briefest in state history. When Bashford arrived at the Capitol to assume office, he brought a contingent of muscular friends. McArthur looked at them and asked, "Will force be used?" "I presume no force will be necessary," Bashford replied, and McArthur beat a hasty retreat amid the jeers and hoots of Republican onlookers.

But Bashford turned out to be just as corrupt as the Democrat he'd beaten. In exchange for favors, he accepted bribes totaling more than $50,000 from railroad promoters. He was not alone—seventy-two legislators also collected bribes from corporations—but after he was exposed in 1858, he chose not to seek re-election.

By then, Wisconsin's original capitol was showing its age. "It was, even for its time, a shoddy structure," Madison pioneer Elisha Keyes recollected, "and all the patching and repairing that was done could not make it very substantial or convenient." The building was being worn down by public officials, and two decades of freezing winters, sweltering summers, and a leaking roof (not to mention a herd of pigs in the basement) had all taken their toll.

In January 1857, Governor Bashford voiced concern about the Capitol's safety in his annual address to lawmakers. "The unsafe condition, in case of fire," he said, "of the records pertaining to the School Land office, merits your serious consideration. All the records of the various state offices, are in like danger of destruction. Some provision should be made, by which our records should be rendered more secure."

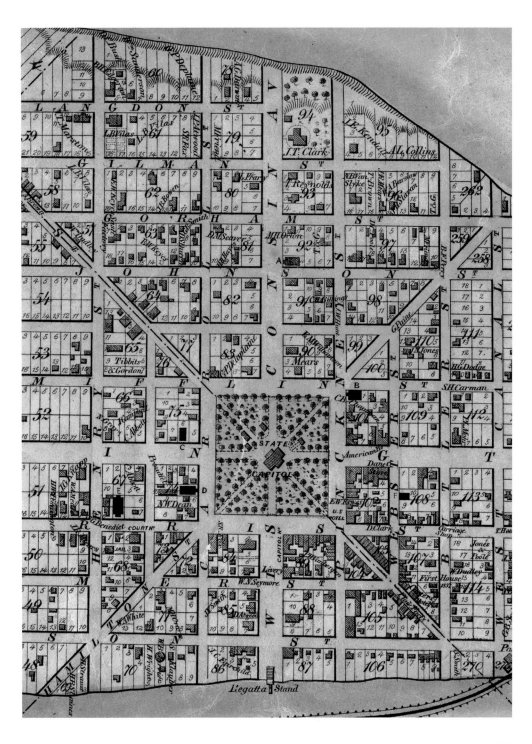

View of the new STATE CAPITOL at MADISON, Wisconsin.
DONNEL & KUTZBOCK Arch! Madison.

Lithograph of the proposed new capitol in 1857, showing Kutzbock's modest dome

WHI IMAGE ID 10023

Some legislators responded by demanding that the state capital be moved and a new building erected in Milwaukee. This prompted Madison city councilors to quickly put up $50,000 to enlarge the existing capitol and keep it where it was. Their offer was supplemented with state funds, and Governor Bashford signed a renovation bill on February 28, 1857, just six weeks after he pointed out the problem.

The state hired local architect August Kutzbock to design the addition. He drew up plans for a large semicircular wing to join the eastern side of the building, and state officials accepted an absurdly low bid to construct it. But one year later, little progress had been made, and an investigation concluded that there was no way to finish the work on time or on budget. So legislators authorized funding for Kutzbock to replace the entire building with a new one.

The multi-phase project took a decade, during which the country fought a civil war and multiple governors and presidents came and went. The legislature moved into a new east wing of the building in 1859, and the last portions of Doty's Washbowl came down in 1863. Work stalled in 1866 when lawmakers insisted that the new dome had to resemble the one on the recently completed US Capitol in Washington, DC. Kutzbock protested that such a large dome would spoil his whole concept for the building and refused to include it. When lawmakers wouldn't budge, he resigned and legislators hired local architect Stephen Vaughan Shipman to complete the project. The huge new dome was well underway in November 1868 when Kutzbock walked out to the end of Picnic Point, took a last look at his ruined masterpiece across the water, and drowned himself in Lake Mendota.

Madison's second capitol was twice the size of its first, measuring 228 feet by 226 feet and rising 225.5 feet above the downtown terrain. Workers finished the exterior walls in light-colored sandstone and constructed four stories of offices and meeting rooms inside, enough to accommodate all state employees. The offices of the governor, secretary of state, and attorney general were on the ground floor; the supreme court, senate, and assembly chambers, and Wisconsin Historical Society were on the second; and the upper floors were filled with galleries, committee rooms, and storage. A thousand-foot-deep well provided the building with fresh water.

During the years of this second capitol's construction, the country was torn apart. After Abraham Lincoln was elected in the fall of 1860, Southern states withdrew from the nation in order to protect their alleged right to enslave African Americans. When hostilities broke out the next spring and Lincoln called for soldiers to enlist, three times as many Wisconsin residents volunteered as could be accommodated. The state eventually furnished more than ninety thousand soldiers to the war, twelve thousand of whom died.

Wisconsin's seventh governor, Louis Harvey, was one of the war's casualties. On April 6, 1862, Wisconsin troops were the first to discover the Confederates' plans for a surprise attack at Shiloh, Tennessee. In the two days of fighting that followed, more American soldiers were killed or wounded than in all of the nation's previous wars combined. News quickly reached Madison that more than six hundred of the state's wounded young men were lying neglected in makeshift tents or on hospital ships. On April 10, Governor Harvey rushed south with a team of Wisconsin doctors and ninety crates of medical supplies.

Harvey visited soldiers in hospitals, on ships, in private homes, and in camps. The governor was a celebrity, and while the physicians treated soldiers' wounds, his presence raised their spirits. By April 19, the supplies had been distributed, and Harvey turned homeward. At 11:00 p.m. that night, while stepping from one steamboat to another in the rain, Harvey slipped and fell into the river. The current was strong, and he never resurfaced. His body was later recovered sixty-five miles downstream.

First Lady Cordelia Harvey was at the Capitol when the news reached Madison. "An attempt was made to get her to her boarding place before the contents of the dispatch were made known," the press reported. "Adjutant-General Gaylord and Mr. Sawyer, her brother-in-law, attempted to accompany her home, and told her that a rumor had been received that gave him some anxiety in regard to the Governor. As Gen. Gaylord was attempting to conceal the full extent of the calamity, she stopped while they were walking through the Park and said: 'Tell me if he is dead!' While he evaded a direct reply, she read the fatal news in the expression of his face and dropped senseless upon the walk."

Another Wisconsin figure made famous during the Civil War was an eagle called Old Abe. Soldiers brought Abe with them into battle, and after the war, he lived in a cage at the Capitol and became a popular tourist attraction.

George Driggs of Fond du Lac described the importance of the eagle in 1864, while the war was still raging: "'Old Abe' is the

Opposite: The second Capitol dome under construction, showing the workmen and the equipment they used to hoist construction materials into place

WHI IMAGE ID 23183

name given to the 'Live Eagle' carried by the Eighth Regiment
Wisconsin Veteran Volunteers. . . . A perch was built for him of
shield shape, with the stars and stripes painted thereon, to which
he is attached by a small rope, giving him liberty of his limbs and
wings for a distance of several yards. . . . The regiment has become
so attached to him, by his long habitation with us, that, rather
than lose him, or see him fall into the hands of the enemy, every
man would spend his last cartridge in his defence. [Confederate]
General [Sterling] Price has been said to declare that he would
rather 'capture that bird than a whole brigade.'"

On October 3, 1862, while the battle raged at Corinth,
Mississippi, the string that held Abe to his perch was cut by
a bullet and he soared aloft over the lines, inspiring the Union

troops; some claimed that he returned with a Confederate cap in his beak. Old Abe survived thirty-seven engagements.

After the war ended, the Eighth Infantry donated him to the government of Wisconsin, and Old Abe spent his postwar years living at the Capitol, attending political rallies and being displayed at charity fundraisers. When a small fire broke out in the basement of the Capitol in 1881, the smoke damaged his health and he died a few weeks later. His body was stuffed and he continued to grace the Capitol until his remains burned in the fire of 1904.

While Old Abe was getting used to his new home at the Capitol, the Wisconsin Supreme Court finally settled the question of African American suffrage. In 1848, the new state constitution had called for a referendum on whether black citizens should be allowed to vote. Balloting took place on November 6, 1849, and Wisconsin voters approved the idea 5,625 to 4,075. But, because there were several other questions on the ballot that day and 5,625 was not a majority of all votes cast on all questions, officials willfully misinterpreted the numbers and claimed the referendum had not passed. In a second referendum in 1857, when the state and nation were divided over the issue of slavery, the voters (all of them white males, by definition) rejected black suffrage and local officials once again refused to let African Americans register to vote.

However, a thirty-three-year-old black man named Ezekiel Gillespie attempted to vote anyway. Born into slavery in Tennessee in 1818, Gillespie had moved to Milwaukee by 1851, where he opened a grocery store and worked for railroad magnate Alexander Mitchell. Gillespie tried to register in every election held in Milwaukee but was always turned away. In 1865, he sued the city for violating his right to vote.

Gillespie's attorney, Byron Paine, had defended the abolitionist Sherman Booth when the latter violated the Fugitive Slave Act in 1854. Paine had also served on the Wisconsin Supreme Court before becoming a Civil War colonel. During the war, he was court-martialed for refusing to return escaped slaves to their

Undated portrait of Ezekiel Gillespie

WHI IMAGE ID 33362

A view of Madison from across Lake Monona in 1884 shows the second Madison capitol in the distance.

WHI IMAGE ID 102418

owners in Louisiana. Paine took Gillespie's case, returned to his old chambers at the Capitol, and set about proving that the 1849 referendum results had been misconstrued. He argued that the majority vote on the single suffrage question satisfied the constitutional requirement and that African Americans had been illegally denied their right to vote for sixteen years. His former colleagues on the state's highest court agreed, and local officials were forced to comply. In the spring 1866 election, Gillespie and

other black Milwaukee residents braved angry curses from racist onlookers to vote for the first time.

The dream of democracy in Wisconsin had moved a bit closer to reality. It would soon be put to the test, however, as a single party grew to dominate state government to a degree not seen before or since. "Power tends to corrupt," a Victorian politician reflected at the time, "and absolute power corrupts absolutely." Wisconsin residents were about to learn this lesson for themselves.

Grand Army of the Republic.

To all unto whom these Presents come, Greeting:

Know Ye, *That reposing full trust and confidence in the fidelity and patriotism of Comrades*

Edgar Richmond.	M. A. Barry.	Thomas Malone.	Frank Tirrill.
John Yule.	William McIntosh.	John R. Scott.	Eben R. Dunlap.
Sidney Wells.	J. A. Wieting.	William Cleland.	John E. Mandeville.
Richard K. Brown.	Byron Waffle.	J. W. Chrisler.	George Phinney.
John Buchanan.	Geo. W. Fenno.	E. C. Johnson.	Robert Steele.
John M. Lewis.	Ira A. Sowders.	Joseph R. Collin.	E. Howard Irwin.
Stephen Clements.	Henry Ballier.	Thomas Strangeway.	James Weast.
N. C. Skelton.	Frank Austin.	J. C. Brown.	John Knutesen.
	Saml. A. Holdridge.		Henry Schlosser.

I do hereby, in Conformity with the Rules and Regulations of the Grand Army of the Republic, and by virtue of the power and authority in me vested, constitute them and their associates and successors a Post of the Grand Army of the Republic, to be known as George H. Irwin *Post No.* twenty five.

Department of Wisconsin

And I authorize and empower them to perform all acts necessary to conduct said organization in accordance with the Rules and Regulations of the Grand Army of the Republic

Dated at the Head Quarters of the Department *of the Grand Army of the Republic at* Waukesha *on the* 19th *day of* March *in the year of our Lord One thousand and Eight hundred and* Eighty two *and of our Independence the One hundred and* sixth.

H. L. Ewest

Department Commander.

Fred M. Kelmer

Ass't Adjutant General.

3

SCHEMERS AND DREAMERS

Life at the Capitol changed dramatically after the Civil War. When the war ended, more than seventy thousand soldiers returned home to Wisconsin. Most of them joined the Grand Army of the Republic (GAR), a veterans' organization that served as a key organizing tool for the Republican Party. Nearly every ambitious, intelligent young veteran joined the GAR and became a Republican. Democrats, who had typically opposed the war or even supported the South, were discredited in Wisconsin for nearly a century. Before the war, several parties and special interests had always wrestled for control of the Capitol. For decades after the war, Wisconsin was a one-party state.

From 1865 to 1895, the Capitol was run by a political machine that hand-picked every candidate, doled out campaign money,

Opposite: Certificate creating Post Number 25,
Department of Wisconsin, of the Grand Army of the Republic

gave away government jobs, awarded state contracts, and wrote every law. An elite handful of state officials, party leaders, and wealthy donors controlled nearly all aspects of Wisconsin politics. They firmly believed, as Calvin Coolidge reportedly said, that "the business of government is business." It was a particularly attractive theory since these officials and their friends owned most of the state's largest businesses.

Their leader was US Senator Philetus Sawyer of Oshkosh, who had made millions in lumbering, railroads, real estate, and banking. Under his leadership, the interests of government and business became synonymous, and influence peddling was a routine way to get things done at the Capitol. For example, all payments to the state government from taxes, invoices, or fees went directly to the state treasurer, who deposited them in the bank. Until they were spent, these deposits earned interest, which the treasurer was allowed to keep for himself.

As difficult as it is to believe today, the state treasurer simply took the interest earned on the state's bank accounts as a supplement to his $1,200 salary—a practice that continued for decades. Since the interest could total $30,000 or more per year, state treasurer was a very desirable job. But to get it, one had to make deals with powerful people. A later investigation revealed that between 1870 and 1890, much of the interest earned on these deposits did not go into the bank account of the incumbent treasurer but into Republican Party coffers.

In 1876, a law was passed prohibiting this practice, but since the officials charged with enforcing it were the same people benefitting from its violation, the law was ignored. During the 1880s, the *Milwaukee Journal* repeatedly demanded investigations, and lawmakers at the Capitol repeatedly denied that there was any need for them. The resulting public outrage helped Democrats into office in 1890. They investigated and brought charges against their Republican predecessors, who fought them all the way to the state supreme court. Research revealed that between 1870 and 1890, a total of $623,444 (the equivalent of over $15 million

Portrait of Senator Philetus Sawyer, ca. 1880

WHI IMAGE ID 30258

today) had been diverted from the state treasury for personal or party use.

Not everyone who worked at the Capitol got rich during this era, though. In fact, supreme court justices were paid so badly that some of them had to borrow money just to make ends meet. The state's 1848 constitution initially set their salaries at $1,500 per year, and a decade later this had risen to $2,500. But the Civil War inflated prices so much that the justices' salaries lost nearly half their value. In 1867, $2,500 bought only as much as $1,450 had a decade earlier.

In 1859, when Chief Justice Luther Dixon arrived in Madison, he was rumored to be "easily worth $15,000." But in a few years, he had spent most of his personal capital just to live in the state's capital. Lucien Hanks was a new teller at the Bank of Madison at the time, and he later recalled helping Dixon out of his financial embarrassment. Chief Justice Dixon approached the bank for a $500 loan, but Hanks was reluctant to grant it because the chief justice had insufficient collateral. Consulting his supervisor, Hanks received permission to give Dixon credit up to $2,000, which was backed confidentially by a sympathetic bank director. Dixon was successfully kept in the dark. When his debt had reached a total of $1,500, he came into the bank and cornered the young teller. "Hanks," he said, "at one time, I did think you were a good banker, but I have now concluded you are a damn-fool; because any man who would loan me $1,500 when I have nothing but my homestead is not competent to be in the business of banking." After delivering this tirade, Dixon requested an additional $500 loan, which Hanks happily approved.

Despite their meager salaries, supreme court justices had to rule on the state's most important issues. In 1874, they bucked the political machine in the *Attorney General v. Railroads* decision that upheld the government's right to regulate business.

By the 1870s, railroads had come to control much of the state's economy by dictating where and when goods were shipped and how much customers had to pay. In 1874, after farmers

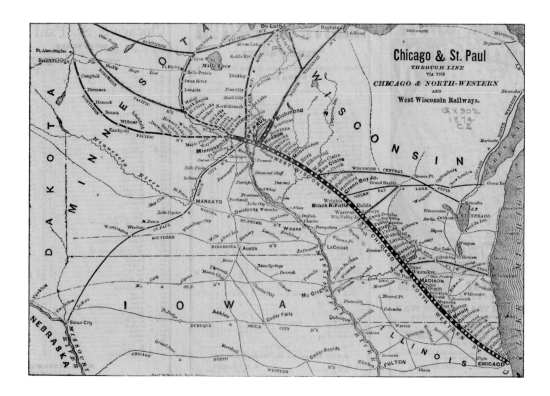

This map shows the Chicago to Saint Paul rail line through Wisconsin by way of the Chicago & North Western and West Wisconsin Railways, ca. 1874.

WHI IMAGE ID 91228

complained bitterly about being squeezed by railroad corporations in order to send their crops to market, lawmakers passed a bill regulating rates and creating a commission to oversee railroad practices. The railroads, naturally, claimed that state government had no right to interfere in their private business, and the case went quickly to the Wisconsin Supreme Court.

In arguments at the Capitol, railroad owners claimed that they'd received corporate charters from the legislature long before this law, which gave them the freedom to charge whatever they wanted and run their businesses however they thought best. They claimed that the new law violated those earlier arrangements. Chief Justice Edward Ryan, however, responded that Wisconsin's constitution not only gave lawmakers the right to issue corporate charters, but also the right to change them. He insisted that preventing state government from regulating businesses would "establish great corporations as independent powers within the

states, a sort of imperia in imperils [empire within an empire],"
which would undermine democratic rule by the people.

His judicial colleagues agreed, and the supreme court ruled
that government possessed broad powers to regulate businesses.
As expected, the next legislature responded by gutting the
powers of the Railroad Commission, but it was a Pyrrhic victory.
The court had laid the cornerstone on which later Progressive
Era laws regulating child labor, working conditions, conservation of natural resources, and many other business regulations
would rest.

Toward the end of the 1870s, another progressive development occurred under the Capitol dome: the assembly hired its
first African American staff member, Benjamin Butts. He became
a fixture at Capitol events and, for fifty years, was a friend of governors and other state officials.

Butts was an eleven-year-old slave when Wisconsin soldiers
liberated his hometown near Petersburg, Virginia, in 1864. He
hung around their camp, and when Colonel Thomas Allen of the
Fifth Wisconsin Infantry asked the orphaned boy if he would like
to do light chores, he accepted the opportunity. When the regiment returned home to Wisconsin, Bennie (as he was known)
followed. He traveled to Richland Center with Major Cyrus
Butt, whose slightly altered surname Bennie adopted, a practice
common among many formerly enslaved people after the war.
His former comrades found work for him to do until he was old
enough to live on his own.

Butts moved to Madison in about 1870. The city had very few
black residents at that time, and prejudice was universal. Personal
services like shaving and cutting hair were among the few jobs
open to African Americans, and Butts found work in a barber shop.
In 1872, while he was still a teenager, he opened his own barber
shop at 5 Pinckney Street, across from the Capitol. "He shaved
daily many notables from the Capitol," recalled a journalist years
later. "Governors Rusk, Washburn, Taylor, Smith, Fairchild and
Peck were among his best customers."

In 1877, in addition to running his own shop, Butts was hired as a washroom attendant for the state assembly, becoming the only black person on the assembly's staff. For many years he also worked as a doorman or butler at official government ceremonies.

"A public function was not complete without Bennie," recalled one acquaintance. "His manners were superb," said another, a remark tinged with the condescension that black people faced every day in turn-of-the-twentieth-century Madison. In 1895, Butts was one of only forty-one African Americans in the city.

In the fall of 1900, the Wisconsin Historical Society moved out of the Capitol to a grand new building on the University of Wisconsin campus and Butts went along. Since the Society's library also served legislators and state officials, it was essential to have someone on its staff who knew his way around the Capitol to deliver and retrieve communications. The middle-aged Butts, who was well-known and well-liked throughout the city, was hired as a messenger. He held the position for three decades.

During these post–Civil War years at the Capitol, probably no one typified the state's Republican leaders better than Governor Jeremiah "Uncle Jerry" Rusk. Rusk was a semi-educated frontier youth when he moved from Ohio to Vernon County. Popular among his farming neighbors, he was elected county sheriff in 1855, coroner in 1857, and state representative in 1862. After leading the Fifteenth Infantry during the Civil War, Rusk joined the GAR in 1866 and was appointed bank comptroller of Wisconsin. During the 1870s, he was elected to Congress and chosen as state commander of the GAR. With the loyal backing of members in its four hundred posts around the state, he was elected governor and took office in the Capitol in 1882.

As wealth and power became even more concentrated during the Gilded Age, working-class residents began to demand a bigger share of the pie. Factory workers organized unions and farmers protested railroad monopolies. Public opinion grew increasingly sympathetic to the plight of ordinary people who operated machines, mined ore, and grew food. From his office

Undated studio portrait of Benjamin Butts

WHI IMAGE ID 45156

in the Capitol, Rusk, whose power came from his popularity in a grassroots veterans' organization, had to maintain a delicate balance between Republican power brokers at the top of Wisconsin society and the masses of common people at the bottom.

Just after Rusk took office in January 1882, 1,700 construction workers were transported to the North Woods to build a rail line out of Superior. When the railroad company suddenly declared bankruptcy, its executives simply abandoned the men in the forest. The angry workers marched into town demanding their wages and threatening to riot. Superior's terrified business leaders, unable to cope with more than a thousand angry laborers "who have neither money nor means of subsistence," frantically telegraphed the Capitol to request military support.

Rusk curtly replied, "These men need bread, not bullets," and refused to call out the troops. Instead, he shipped food to the workers and promised to secure their back wages if they remained calm. Then he quickly finessed through the legislature a bill allowing a new corporation to buy out the failed one—but only if it first paid the $78,000 owed to the workers. Over the next three years, Rusk refused to use force to put down strikes in Superior and Eau Claire, earning him a reputation as "a friend of the workingman." But four years later, he turned into their enemy.

The Milwaukee Labor Reform Association, with other groups around the nation, had begun to demand an eight-hour work day. The group began a two-year campaign on May 1, 1886, and within a week, striking workers had shut down all of the city's industrial plants except one—the North Chicago Railroad Rolling Mills Steel Foundry in Bay View. Similar marches and strikes were upsetting the status quo in Baltimore, Chicago, and Cleveland. In Milwaukee, a crowd of demonstrators marched to Bay View on May 5 to convince its workers to join the strike.

Hundreds of protesters surrounded the steel foundry while others paraded through the city's streets. Anxious Milwaukee leaders asked Governor Rusk to send in troops to save the city from anarchy, and this time he did. National Guard soldiers

Newspaper cartoon of Jeremiah Rusk, 1892

WHI IMAGE ID 107657

A colored lithograph of the Capitol from the *1872 Wisconsin Blue Book*

WHI IMAGE ID 23403

promptly arrived at Bay View and fired into the crowd. Five unarmed demonstrators and onlookers were shot dead and four were wounded. Rusk reportedly commented, "I seen my duty and I done it." His remark was quoted in newspapers all over the country and carried him out of the Capitol in Madison and into the corridors of power in Washington, where he served in President Benjamin Harrison's cabinet.

Under this long period of Republican rule, Wisconsin's government exploded in size, and the Capitol built in 1857 could no longer house all the state's employees. By 1880, nearly thirty departments, boards, commissions, and other offices had been created. A State Board of Immigration tried to attract new workers, a Board of Public Lands sold farms, a Railroad Commission kept goods moving, educators ran state schools and colleges, judges and clerks staffed sixteen courts, timber agents and lumber inspectors and even fish commissioners watched over natural resources, and a state militia was kept ready to maintain order. The printed list of state officers grew from just three pages in the 1854 *Blue Book* (the biennial guide to state government) to twenty-four pages in the 1883 book.

Faced with overcrowding under the dome, the legislature of 1882 appropriated $200,000 to expand the Capitol with two large extensions to its North and South Wings. These were to give new quarters to the supreme court, the Wisconsin Historical Society, the State Library, and legislative staffs, and enable reshuffling of the other departments. When bids came in, however, they all exceeded the budget of $200,000 and were rejected. A second round of bidding fared better, but after selecting the lowest bid, lawmakers pruned the budget back even further. During 1883, under the guidance of contractors John Bentley and Oscar Nowlan and architect D. R. Jones, two tall additions rose up on the north and south ends of the building.

But cutting the budget of the lowest bidder had predictable and tragic results on the quality of the work. After lunch on November 8, 1883, the entire city was stunned as the Capitol's new South Wing came crashing down, causing a thunderous boom that rolled a mile in every direction and sent an immense cloud of white dust into the sky.

Thirty workers lay screaming beneath the pile of stone and rubble. Others hung from twisted girders five stories above the wreckage, their blood trailing down the Capitol's walls. Bystanders and downtown residents rushed into the ruins as the dust clouds were still spreading and desperately tried to rescue the buried victims.

Sixteen-year-old Frank Lloyd Wright was on his way home from a UW–Madison engineering class and passed by the Capitol just as it collapsed. "Men with bloody faces came plunging wildly out of the basement entrance," he recalled. "Someone pointed to a hand sticking out between chunks of brick-work on which the crowd itself was standing. After pulling away bricks, finally scarlet plaster, a mangled human being was drawn out—too late. . . . And

The ruins of the unfinished South Wing of the Capitol after its collapse in 1883

WHI IMAGE ID 5021

so it went on all day long and far into the night." When Wright finally made it home after dark, he had nightmares and claimed in later years that the horror of the scene never entirely left him.

Five workers were killed and twenty others severely injured. The media pounced on the architects and builders for negligence, and two investigations started. One, called by Governor Rusk, found that substandard materials had been used in the main supporting columns, which gave way under the weight of the upper floors. The second, initiated by the coroner's jury, included Dane County District Attorney Robert La Follette, fresh out of UW Law School and at the very start of his political career. The jury called several injured workmen as witnesses, who reported inch-wide cracks in the basement walls, crumbling bricks, and ad hoc efforts to jack up the girders to hide the defects.

The court found contractors Bentley and Nowlan and architect Jones guilty of negligence, but none of them were seriously punished. In fact, Bentley and Nowlan were rehired to clean up the mess and finish erecting the new wing, which they completed a year later, in November 1884. The newly expanded capitol stretched 226 feet east to west, 396 feet north to south, and towered 225 feet above downtown Madison. Its general shape was that of a cross, with two corridors intersecting at the rotunda under the dome.

Though it may be hard to imagine today, the Capitol was an exclusively male club until the late 1880s. Not only were all elected officials men, but state employees were all men, too. The list of staff in the *Wisconsin Blue Book* includes every clerk and janitor and washroom attendant, but it's impossible to find a woman's name listed there until typewriters were introduced during the 1880s.

In 1880, there were only six thousand typists and stenographers in the whole country, and most of them were men. But by the decade's end, there were thirty-three thousand, and most of them were women. A few years later, nine out of ten typing jobs were held by women. Women flocked to secretarial work because it was a high-level technical skill that paid approximately ten times more than they could earn in factories or as domestic servants. Employers were thrilled to have women typists because they could be paid less than men. Also, the new technology enabled far more work to get done in the same amount of time, so Wisconsin officials began to employ female office workers.

The first woman to work in the Capitol may have been Winona Merrick, who started in 1887 in the Department of Public Instruction, inspecting and certifying the credentials of new teachers. In the early 1890s, Mary Priestly of Mineral Point began managing records in the Adjutant General's office, which she considered "the next best thing to being a soldier, [which] is what she most wanted to be when she was a child." At least twenty-two women worked at the Capitol by 1900, including

Katherine Houghton, who was responsible for cutting fifteen thousand checks a month to meet the state's payroll and pay its bills. Ten women (nearly half of those under the Capitol dome at the turn of the century) worked in the Wisconsin Historical Society as editors, researchers, or librarians.

Like all state workers, these pioneering women were at risk of being arbitrarily dismissed whenever a new administration was voted in. But they also had to face insults and condescension from male coworkers and supervisors. "At first," wrote Robert La Follette in 1912, "even in our own camp, there was some opposition to the appointment of women in the state service—a survival of the old political belief that 'the boys ought to have the places.'" One Capitol visitor remarked on the "rare presence of mind and

Elevated view of the Capitol shortly after the construction of the North and South additions

WHI IMAGE ID 3474

self-control" displayed by a female lobbyist in the face of sarcastic comments from assemblymen during a 1915 suffrage discussion.

Many of the women working at the Capitol in the late nineteenth century were among the first female graduates of the University of Wisconsin. Some of them worked for the state until World War II, dedicating their entire lives to public service. After women won the right to vote in 1920, their numbers increased in state government, but a woman was not elected to statewide office until 1960, and a woman did not appear on the supreme court until 1976.

Another first for the Capitol came in 1890 when Wisconsin elected a professional humorist as its governor. George Peck was a Milwaukee journalist who wrote short fiction about a

Two Historical Society librarians, Minnie Oakley and Florence Baker Hayes, at work in 1896

WHI IMAGE ID 23281

precociously naughty "Bad Boy" who plagued his father with practical jokes. Peck's comic tales swept the nation and he became a celebrity. When he entered politics, he'd just published a Civil War memoir, *How Private George W. Peck Put Down the Rebellion*, which he described as "reminiscences of the ridiculous part taken in the struggle, by a raw recruit, who was too scared to fight and too frightened to run." As an editor, he railed against the waste of state money on boondoggles, such as a bill passed to give incentives for inventing early automobiles: "It is such legislation that makes people swear," he wrote. "The state didn't need a steam mule any more than a dog needs two tails."

At the 1890 Wisconsin Democratic convention, Peck was introduced as "a humorous and cheerful writer, one who tried to throw sunshine and happiness around the path of hardship and toil"—hardly a recommendation for someone trying to find employment in the devious, in-fighting, backbiting world of Gilded Age politics. Much to everyone's surprise, he won the popular vote and became one of only two Democrats to occupy the executive office between 1856 and 1933.

Peck's two terms under the Capitol dome during the 1890s were relatively uneventful. One reporter remembered him as "a man of high integrity who was more adept as a speaker, writer, and companion than as a Governor." He wasn't going to throw a wrench into the gears of the well-oiled political machine that had run state government from smoky backrooms for decades. That would have to wait for an inspired crusader willing to play David against the Republican Goliath.

Peck was not the only joker at the Capitol at this time. One day during his administration, a legislator rolled his eyes at a colleagues' endless monologue and found himself staring at the ceiling, which gave him a brilliant idea.

When the second capitol was finished in 1869, its assembly chamber featured an enormous chandelier. This was before electric lighting, and the massive fixture took an entire hour to light by hand and another hour to extinguish. As the years passed, this chandelier grew rickety and unstable. Lawmakers felt nervous sitting under it. So, around 1890, it was taken down, leaving a wide hole in the ceiling. Piled high around the edges of this hole was a decades-old accumulation of soot and dust, deep enough to shovel.

Sometime after 1890, the bored lawmaker secretly ordered a Capitol page to climb into the crawl space above the ceiling and position a heavy plank beside the hole. One end of the plank was propped up by a stick, and from the stick a cord descended into a closet just outside the assembly chamber. The next day, as a member of the opposing party was droning on and on, the lawmaker slipped into the closet and jerked the rope. The plank came

Portrait of George W. Peck when he was a Democratic candidate for governor of Wisconsin

Legislators in the assembly chamber in 1899

crashing down in the crawl space, sending a shower of dust cascading over the assembly that ended the day's proceedings.

Instead of denouncing the perpetrator, lawmakers decided to pay a Capitol page $2.50 a day to keep the trap ready. Any member could sneak out and pull the cord at any moment. Some legislators brought umbrellas to assembly debates. Whenever a representative left the chamber, everyone instantly perked up. Speeches became shorter, voting went faster, and the people's business was conducted more efficiently.

It was during this decade that Wisconsin legislators passed the state's civil rights law, seventy years ahead of the US Congress. It was created when the state's African American residents got fed up with discrimination and mobilized their political power.

In September 1889, Owen Howell, a black resident of Milwaukee, was denied his seat after purchasing a ticket at the Bijou Opera House. The city's black community numbered about five hundred people at the time, and most of them attended a public meeting in November that launched a lawsuit by Howell against the theater owner. They protested that the opera house, while discriminating against black customers, would happily admit "a drunkard, a gambler, a thief or a prostitute, provided the skin was white." An all-white jury found in favor of Howell, awarding him $100 in damages plus court costs.

The meeting leaders also decided to call for an explicit civil rights law. This was controversial, because the US Supreme Court had just declared a federal civil rights act unconstitutional in 1883 and ruled that racial discrimination was perfectly legal. In other states, civil rights laws were being rolled back, not expanded. But Wisconsin's African American residents were angry. Frederick Douglass had been denied a room at a Janesville hotel. Black Civil War veterans had been turned away from Milwaukee hotels during GAR conferences. African American teachers had been denied accommodations at a Madison convention.

Governor William Hoard, a Republican, supported a civil rights bill. "Wisconsin should not be behind any of the states in guaranteeing to the colored people all of those rights given them by the constitution," he told the media. A bill penalizing business owners for discriminating on the basis of race was submitted in January 1891 by Milwaukee representative Orren Williams. However, it was watered down in the assembly and rejected by the senate after blatantly racist debates at the Capitol.

Among those testifying in support of the bill in January was young William T. Green of Milwaukee, the first African American graduate of the University of Wisconsin Law School. A few months later, his neighbors chose him as a delegate to the 1892 Wisconsin Republican convention, where he gave a passionate speech and persuaded the party to insert civil rights into its platform. When Republicans regained control of the state legislature in 1894, they passed the civil rights bill. It guaranteed equal treatment at inns, restaurants, and a long list of other public places; violators could be fined from $5 to $100 or receive six months in jail. The law was quickly challenged, but the Wisconsin Supreme Court upheld it, and racial discrimination in public accommodations became illegal in Wisconsin. Which is not to say, of course, that it ended.

The inevitable public clash between the Republican oligarchs who ran the Capitol's political machine and impatient young reformers finally occurred around the turn of the century thanks to a cow. Governor Edward Scofield, who was elected in 1896, was a farm boy and didn't like Madison's big-city milk. So he had his favorite cow shipped to the capital by rail—without paying for it.

Free rides were commonplace at the time, especially for lawmakers and party officials. By handing out free passes, the railroads ingratiated themselves with legislators who controlled the rates they could charge. Railroads even provided extra passes for politicians to hand out as incentives for undecided voters or as rewards for supporters. In return, the railroad corporations generally got whatever they wanted from their friends in government.

But Robert M. La Follette considered the free passes nothing less than bribery, calling them "a great asset of the machine politicians" that "went far toward corrupting the politics of the state." La Follette had graduated from the UW in 1879 and had quickly been elected Dane County district attorney, where he irritated the old guard with his views on clean government. He served in Congress from 1884 to 1890, when he lost re-election during the Democratic wave that brought Governor Peck to the Capitol.

He returned to practice law in Madison, and when he was hired to prosecute the state treasurer for illegally using state funds for personal and party purposes, he claimed that Senator Philetus Sawyer offered him a bribe to settle the case. "[This] brought the whole system home to me personally in its ugliest and most revolting form," La Follette wrote afterward, and he devoted his career to building his own movement to defeat the political machine. But whenever La Follette and his allies at the Capitol tried to outlaw free railroad passes, they were blocked by the old guard—that is, until Governor Scofield's cow rode the rails.

The upstart progressives quickly pointed out to Wisconsin farmers and factory workers that, while they were required to pay full fares out of their hard-earned wages, small-time political operatives and even a lowly cow were getting free rides. "It raised a storm of mingled ridicule and resentment," La Follette recalled. "Scofield's cow became famous, her picture appeared in the newspapers, and she came to be known in every home in the state."

During the legislative session of 1899, the progressives' reform bill finally passed and, in La Follette's words, "at once cut off one of the strong props of the boss system in Wisconsin." It was the first crack in the armor of the corrupt political machine that had controlled Wisconsin since the Civil War.

Another high-profile Capitol controversy from the 1890s revolved around women's underwear. Representative Henry Daggett of Bear Creek, in rural Waupaca County, thought young women should be stopped from wearing clothing that accentuated their tiny waists. Contemporary feminists argued that tight corsets were unhealthy, but Daggett acted not to safeguard women's health but to purify public morals. He told the press that "for years he has studied the figures of the ladies of Bear Creek" and "the waists of most ladies are about half the size they should be."

So in January 1899, Daggett introduced a bill outlawing tight corsets. It was first referred to the Assembly Committee on Public Improvements, who passed it quickly to the Committee of Public Health and Sanitation, who handed it off like a hot potato to the Committee of Agriculture. Some lawmakers protested that the legislature had more important issues to address than regulating women's fashion. Others felt that the fit of the underwear an individual chose to wear was no business of the government's.

Portrait of Robert M. La Follette Sr. at age twenty-nine when he was elected to Congress in 1884

Outside the Capitol, people laughed at Daggett. He was ridiculed for prudishness in the Janesville, Oshkosh, and Chicago papers. At one Madison party, a large painting was hung showing him as a medieval knight, sword in hand, ready to battle a monstrous corset. When he shipped his trunk home at the end of the session, it arrived pasted over with pictures of scantily clad, tightly corseted women, raising eyebrows at the Bear Creek train depot. This was too much for Daggett, who let his resolution die quietly in committee.

"Fighting Bob" La Follette had more important things on his mind than how women chose to wear their undergarments. He'd prosecuted the corrupt state treasurers in 1891 and ended railroad pass bribery in 1899. He focused next on ensuring that candidates were actually chosen by voters, rather than party bosses.

Wisconsin voters had technically never chosen their top elected officials. They simply sanctioned whomever the party bosses put on the ballot. "Wherever there was a close contest in a nominating convention," recalled Senator Irvine Lenroot, "those who were willing to bribe delegates seldom failed to find some who were willing to be bribed." Wisconsin was a one-party state where candidates were named in secret by a handful of men who controlled the government, the economy, and the media.

In 1897, La Follette called for direct primary elections to replace this corrupt system. For years, he was thwarted by the incumbents who profited from it, but in 1903 he marshaled enough allies to force a statewide referendum. Fearing that the old guard would undermine it at the next state Republican convention, La Follette hired UW football players to work security. Every delegate had to show proper credentials and run a gauntlet of tough guys to get in. Reform carried the day, and in the November 1904 referendum, voters endorsed the change from secret caucuses to open primaries.

But when the first direct primary was held in 1906, La Follette got a surprise. He had hand-picked Irvine Lenroot to succeed him as governor and aligned progressive leaders behind him. The

Caryl Fairchild, daughter of Governor Lucius Fairchild, wearing a corset beneath her dress in 1896

WHI IMAGE ID 34350

voters, however, chose incumbent governor James O. Davidson to be the Republican candidate instead. The system worked, and not even La Follette himself could control it.

La Follette's election as governor in 1900 launched an optimistic period at the Capitol, when Republicans who embraced Lincoln's vision of a "government of the people, by the people, and for the people" generally prevailed over the former political machine. These so-called progressive Republicans believed it was right and proper for government to help common citizens deal with challenges like poverty, disease, unemployment, and injustice. To do this, lawmakers needed accurate, comprehensive information about social problems and legal experts to draft bills that would address them.

Most legislators were small-town businessmen or farmers with very little experience in the law. Until then, new bills had usually been written and pushed through by lobbyists on behalf of special interests. During La Follette's first term, in 1901, Wisconsin lawmakers created a Legislative Reference Bureau, the first agency in the nation designed to provide a state legislature with competent, professional help. They hired a young librarian, Charles McCarthy, to run it.

McCarthy was the son of poor immigrants in Boston; he ran away to sea as a boy and later worked as a carpenter. "He came to Brown University," a former professor wrote, "as a wild Irish lad of the roughest appearance, the son of a mechanic in Brockton [Massachusetts], and at first appeared to be chiefly a football player." He went on to earn his PhD at Madison, where he coached the UW football team. His passion for the Badgers earned

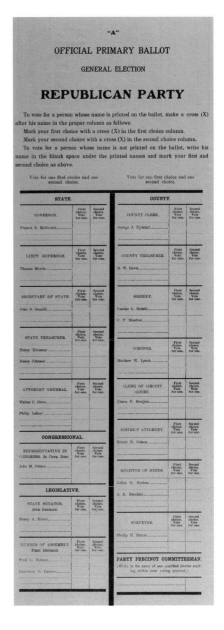

Official primary ballot for the Republican Party on Tuesday, September 3, 1912

WHI IMAGE ID 34239

Dr. Charles R. McCarthy
and staff at the
Legislative Reference
Library in 1906

him the loyalty of thousands of alumni, who stood by him as he began to turn Wisconsin government upside down.

McCarthy's idea was that the ill-equipped lawmakers should have ready access to reliable facts and university-trained experts. He intended that the people of Wisconsin should be governed by laws drafted in their interest through a well-informed, carefully reasoned, and nonpartisan process. His library not only supplied relevant research and information to lawmakers, but his staff also drafted the text of laws on a host of social, economic, and political issues. The notion of having unbiased, university-trained experts draft bills rather than lobbyists or party hacks was a radical notion at the time. It became known as part of "the Wisconsin Idea" after McCarthy published a book with that title in 1912.

From their Capitol offices, McCarthy and his staff researched, drafted, and helped enact laws providing for direct primary elections, safer factories, worker's compensation, regulation of big corporations, limited working hours for women and children, environmental conservation, state parks, public libraries, public health services, and the formation of the University of Wisconsin Extension system. Some of these passed while La Follette was governor, between 1901 and 1906, but most were enacted under Governors James Davidson and Francis McGovern between 1906 and 1914. During the 1930s, ideas hatched under the Capitol dome by McCarthy's staff and protégés were embodied in New Deal programs such as the 1935 Social Security Act. In fact, the momentum of Wisconsin progressivism rippled down through the decades into John Kennedy's New Frontier and Lyndon Johnson's Great Society programs of the 1960s.

Some people disagreed with these ideas, of course. Many thought they went too far in restricting the freedom of business owners or making government too big. In 1915, conservative Republican Governor Emanuel Philipp introduced legislation to shut down the Legislative Reference Bureau, which he considered merely a progressive bill factory. With tongue firmly planted in cheek, McCarthy testified at its committee hearing that the bill to eliminate his office "as drawn was defective, but that his drafting bureau would gladly put it into proper shape." He also offered to resign, saying he "would enjoy being outside the Capitol throwing bricks through the windows" by becoming a lobbyist. The bill went nowhere, and two years later McCarthy was asked to organize the state's World War I draft process.

When McCarthy died in 1921 from exhaustion and overwork, he left a legacy broader than partisan politics. Today, every state has a department staffed by impartial experts who research and draft bills. And the idea that government should be staffed by pragmatic idealists using scientific knowledge to serve the interests of common people would dominate American politics for the next half century.

4

CREATING A MONUMENT

By 1900, Wisconsin's Capitol had one of the most advanced fire-fighting systems in the nation. Back in 1857, Governor Coles Bashford had highlighted the risk of fire to the first Madison capitol, and lawmakers quickly approved construction of a new fireproof one. Minor blazes that broke out in the decades that followed were quickly extinguished. During the 1890s, a state-of-the-art sprinkler system was installed in the attic above the senate and assembly chambers, water pipes attached to hundreds of feet of hose were installed in each wing, and eleven hydrants were positioned around the Capitol grounds. The building's water supply was hooked up to both the university's reservoir on top of Bascom Hill and, as a backup, to the city's water pipes.

When the building was shut down each night, two small gas lamps were left burning for use by two security guards who patrolled its hallways. Around 2:45 a.m. on February 27, 1904, one of the guards smelled smoke. He traced it to a small flame above one of these gas jets on the second floor of the West Wing, where the ceiling had recently been refinished. He threw buckets of water at the ceiling while his companion ran for the nearest fire hose, unrolled it, and turned the valve. No water came out.

The previous day, workers at the tanks on Bascom Hill had drained the whole system while repairing a university boiler, and the pressure was too low to force water all the way to the Capitol. The overhead pipes in the attic would have failed for the same reason, and the guards never turned them on. The city water supply could be tapped only by city workers, and none were on hand at three in the morning.

So the guards dropped their buckets and called the Madison fire department. The first company of firefighters, mostly volunteers, arrived in a horse-drawn wagon half an hour later, by which time the flames had spread through the ceiling of the West Wing. A second company followed close on their heels, tried

A lithographic portrait of Madison Fire Engine Company #2 posed in front of the newly designed, but as yet unbuilt, Capitol building in 1857

WHI IMAGE ID 1872

unsuccessfully to get water from the university line, and then in desperation ran their hoses down to Lake Monona.

By then, the newly varnished ceiling, the wooden beams above it, the lathe and plaster walls, and the interior furnishings of the West Wing were all ablaze. Fire lit up the sky and flames shot out through the assembly chamber roof and windows. As firefighters plunged bravely into the building, the fire reached a storeroom filled with ammunition. Hundreds of bullets flew through the smoke and flames.

It was a drizzly, foggy night, and an eerie glow greeted fifteen-year-old Joseph Livermore when he looked out his attic window two blocks away, awakened by the fire alarms at about 4:00 a.m. He told an interviewer, "My brother and I popped out of bed and as I dashed out, why there was my little vest pocket Kodak [camera] on the dresser there, and I stuck that in my hip pocket and went out and went up to the fire."

Livermore made his way around to the Capitol's south side, between Main and Pinckney Streets. "Burdick and Murray had a store there with three cast iron steps going up from the sidewalk to the store level, and I set my camera on the top step and gave it a three-minute exposure." The teenager's photograph was the only one taken of the burning capitol, and afterward he sold prints for a nickel each. A con man later talked him out of the negative and printed hundreds of color postcards without sharing any of the sizable profits with the young photographer.

As Livermore watched the fire spread out of control, Governor La Follette was awakened at his home on East Gilman Street. He rushed to the Capitol Square, joined by hundreds of UW students running up State Street and downtown residents dashing from their homes to help. The governor paused briefly to take in the situation and then plunged straight into the inferno.

"He ran everywhere through the burning building," wrote an eyewitness, "directing the work of rescue of valuable records and documents." La Follette helped carry out paintings, furniture, and the archives of state government until two citizens "took him by the arm and dragged him out of the building." Though he was "completely soaked from head to foot," he wouldn't be kept down. After putting on dry clothes, he ran back into the fray.

By 4:30 a.m., it became clear that the emergency was too big for Madison crews to handle by themselves, and fire departments in Milwaukee, Janesville, and other cities were called for help. Milwaukee's fire engine arrived by train in just an hour and a half, but it had to be thawed out before it would work. By 5:00 a.m., the West Wing "looked like one gigantic flame" according to the *Wisconsin State Journal*, and the other wings were also ablaze. Firefighters and their equipment surrounded the building. "I counted at one time, there were 26 pumping outfits going, pumping water from Lake Monona and shooting the hoses on there," Livermore recalled. "And the fire was so intense that with all that water pouring on there it seemed that the water only went up in steam."

Because the smoke was so thick in the stairwells, UW students propped ladders up to the second floor supreme court library and

created a human chain to pass books out, one by one. Clerks in the secretary of state's office waded through the frigid water that had collected from the hoses to rescue legal records. The North Wing was saved thanks to courageous volunteer firefighters who stood their ground until the floor burned out from under them, then ran outside and poured streams of water onto it from above, effectively halting the fire's progress in that direction.

By the time the flames died down around 10:00 a.m., the West and East Wings, the rotunda, and the upper floors of the South Wing were piles of smoking rubble. Only five offices—the supreme court, attorney general, insurance commissioner, Public Lands, and Office of Control—survived intact. The assembly and senate chambers were completely destroyed. The offices of the state treasurer, the secretary of state, the Free Library Commission, and the Grand Army of the Republic were wrecked. The stuffed

View of the senate
chamber after the fire

WHI IMAGE ID 23123

carcass of Old Abe, the eagle that accompanied Wisconsin's
Eighth Regiment during the Civil War, had gone up in flames, too.
In many places, naked cast-iron columns rose like skeletons out
of the ashes. Two firefighters were seriously injured, but, fortu-
nately, no one died in the disaster.

As the afternoon unfolded, thousands of sightseers converged
on the Capitol Square from surrounding towns. Some took photos
and reminisced, while others rooted around in the steaming piles
for souvenirs. Most everyone went home brokenhearted at the
destruction of the state's most important symbol of freedom and
democracy. Firefighters continued their work until 10:00 p.m.,
when the last embers were finally extinguished.

THE WISCONSIN CAPITOL

"Fighting Bob" La Follette was exhausted, and the site of his hopes and dreams lay in ruins. The Capitol where he'd spent years fighting to end corruption, expand democracy, and create a government that truly served the people was a smoldering ruin. A few days later, he wrote to a friend in Washington, "Yes, the old Capitol is sadly changed, and in a few years it will be only a memory, for I have no doubt that the citizens of Wisconsin will insist on having an entirely new building put up in its stead. We need it, surely; nevertheless, I shall regret to see it go, for, as you say, many cherished associations cling about it."

Clean-up crews, meanwhile, had begun shoveling away the rubble and ash. Supporters wrote to donate office space and typewriters. And just four days after the fire, state workers were returning to areas that survived or settling into rented offices across the street. Over the next thirteen years, the Capitol we love today would rise out of the ashes.

Even before the fire, state officials had realized that the old capitol was no longer adequate. The population of the state had grown to more than two million, and more workers than ever before were needed to serve them. Since 1887, the secretary of state's staff had grown from fourteen to twenty-four, the Department of Public Instruction from four to thirteen, and other agencies had expanded in similar proportions. The building had infrastructure problems, too. Although electricity had been installed and the heating and cooling system updated, large sections of the building that had been built before the Civil War were showing their age.

In 1903, lawmakers had authorized a Capitol Improvement Commission to solve overcrowding in the North Wing. After the fire, they faced a much bigger task. They initially sent out a request for proposals (RFP) to repair the building by replacing the burned-out center and erecting replacement wings, but the contractors who responded all agreed that a totally new building was needed. Since the 1903 Improvement Commission had not been authorized to make decisions on that scale, they went back to the legislature for new instructions.

Like most documents written by a committee, the RFP took a long time to hammer out, especially in Wisconsin's highly charged political climate where progressive and mainstream Republicans butted heads on every question. Individual legislators fiddled with minor details of the building specifications, others tried to insert language favoring contractors in their own districts, and some commission members simply resigned in frustration. The commission's smartest move was hiring forty-three-year-old Madison architect Lew Porter to oversee the project.

Porter had founded his own architectural firm in 1885 while he was still a UW undergraduate, and young Frank Lloyd Wright later apprenticed there. Over the next twenty years, Porter personally designed or worked on some of Madison's most striking buildings, including the university's Red Gym and Science Hall, Fauerbach Brewery, many grand private homes, and later, in 1912, the Camp Randall arch. Shortly after the Capitol fire, Porter was hired as a consultant, and in 1906 he agreed to superintend the massive project of building a new capitol.

The commission sent out a second RFP in January 1906, after nearly two years of discussion, deliberation, and recrimination by lawmakers. Porter solicited applications from five of the most prestigious architectural companies in America, including those who had designed monumental buildings for the 1893 World's Columbian Exposition in Chicago and landmarks in New York, Boston, and Washington, DC.

They were asked to submit proposals for "a complete and harmonious plan for a State Capitol Building, including a Dome, to be erected section by section, . . . each section being substantially complete in itself, the number of sections to be five, consisting of four wings and the central or dome portion. . . . The four wings are to be of equal length and area, arranged in the form of a St. Andrews cross."

The RFP filled an oblong-shaped book of nearly forty pages. It was quite detailed, including drawings of acceptable floor plans, specific locations of various rooms and chambers, and even the

Undated portrait of
George B. Post

WHI IMAGE ID 102163

THE WISCONSIN CAPITOL

number and size of the restrooms. One of the most challenging specifications was that the remains of the old building had to be occupied while the new one was being built on the same site. As fast as each new wing was completed, employees were to move into it from their old dilapidated spaces in the ruins, which were then knocked down to make room for the next phase of construction.

The commission received responses from all five firms by the deadline of June 15, 1906, and Porter enlisted his former teacher Allan Conover and Chicago architect Daniel Burnham to help evaluate them. On July 17, 1906, the commission voted unanimously to award the contract to George B. Post & Sons.

Post, a former president of the American Institute of Architects, was known for monumental buildings that pushed the limits of design and engineering. In 1870, he'd built the first office building to use elevators, and he went on to construct the tallest buildings of that era in New York City. He'd also designed the thirty-acre Manufactures and Liberal Arts Building at the World's

George B. Post & Sons' design of the third Madison capitol building

Columbian Exposition, thought at the time to be the largest structure on earth. When his plan for the Capitol was accepted, he'd just finished designing the New York Stock Exchange and begun working on the City College of New York campus.

Post envisioned a monumental, classically inspired capitol that would exude dignity and grandeur. Its cruciform layout would echo European cathedrals, and its conspicuous paintings, statues, and decorations would make it feel like a museum. At the same time, it would function efficiently as an office building thanks to modern technological elements such as electricity, telephones, elevators, a central vacuum cleaning system, and a state-of-the-art ventilation and heating plant. Post was seventy-two years old at the time, and he clearly intended the Wisconsin Capitol to be the crowning glory of his long and distinguished career. Porter looked forward to working with him, and they started immediately.

The exterior of the West Wing was nearing completion in the fall of 1909 when the first death of a construction worker occurred. Work was running behind schedule because the Vermont granite supplier hadn't delivered stone on time. Sculptor Karl Bitter, who'd designed statues to go above the west entrance, was impatient to get them finished before winter. But they couldn't be put in place until the base underneath them was installed. He typically had assistants do rough carving on the ground and then he

The West Wing pediment, called "The Unveiling of the Resources of the State," sculpted by Karl Bitter

personally completed the work after his statues were lifted to their final locations.

Installation of the statues' base was carried out by foreman Dan Logan, "a man always in a hurry," according to his friend William Van Deusen. In this case, Logan was in such a hurry that he ordered his crew to work on Sunday, October 24, 1909, to get work back on schedule. Logan's supervisor knew his habits and cautioned him: "Dan listen!! You go slow erecting that pediment. Bank every stone with due care before you attempt to pile the next stone atop, remember each must balance the following, stone by stone, and bank each securely!!!"

At about three that afternoon, Logan was working eighty feet above the Capitol Square with Frank Bliss, "a boy who grew up with me," Van Deusen recalled, "and who was at that time a young man assisting Logan with the stonework and the banking of each stone as it was put in place." They had built up the base of the pediment to support Bitter's statues and were laying a four-ton piece of granite when the stone beneath it cracked, sending the whole pile cascading down to the street. "Frank saw the beginning of the parting of what was already in place, [and] jumped to safety, but turned and saw Dan go down with that massive stone, statues and all." Logan was killed instantly, but the rest of his crew escaped unharmed.

Stone carvers work
on statue groups that
would be placed at the
exterior base of the
Capitol dome.

71

Porter concluded that the extra weight of the uncarved statuary had caused the accident, and from then on, all sculpting was completed in shacks on the Capitol grounds or at the railroad depot on West Washington Avenue before statues were raised.

Van Deusen also recalled another fatality that happened during construction. "As you may know," he wrote years afterwards to a friend,

> when the steelwork of a building has reached to height there is, or was, a custom of placing an American flag on the highest pinnacle. This was done on the state capitol, that, of course, before the statue was placed on the high point of the dome. This flag-raising was done shortly before the Fourth of July (year I forget). During the Fourth of July, one of the workmen, who was celebrating and filled himself to a good capacity with liquor, against much warning, climbed inside to the innermost part of the dome, which at that time was far from completion, that is, stonework—marble—painting etc. etc.

Workmen demolish the North Wing in 1913.

WHI IMAGE ID 4899

When well up, he lost his balance and fell to the lower floor. En route down, his body snapped cross-supporting rods 1 inch and 1½ inch thick, so you can see the speed going down accepted no interference. Naturally he never lived to tell the tale and before his final stop he was a goner.

As the project's superintendent, Lew Porter tolerated no corner-cutting or shoddiness from his workers, partly because he wanted to prevent these types of accidents. He was compulsively vigilant about every detail in the specifications. Van Deusen remembered that "whatever the plan called for was carefully checked," and Porter's correspondence is full of angry missives forcing contractors to live up to their promises.

One place where Porter deviated from the specified plan, though, was in the Capitol toilet seats. Legislators had recently passed a sanitary law requiring public restrooms to use toilet seats shaped like those we see today, with a gap in the front of the oval. Before this law, public toilet seats were cut in a complete circle, which was considered more likely to spread disease. Somewhere in architect George Post's office, an underling had specified the traditional full-circle toilet seats for the Capitol. "Someone called the newspapers attention," recalled Van Deusen, "and it got in print. . . . Of course, there the specifications were wrong. But when the newspaper aroused the public, enough said—the change was made. No fault in a way of Mr. Porter."

As that anecdote shows, the Capitol was planned in scrupulous detail. Post's staff spent thousands of hours designing furnishings, fixtures, finishes, and hardware, and Porter spent many more to make sure subcontractors completed their work according to those specifications. This even included the Capitol cuspidors, or spittoons.

Cynics have suggested for centuries that politicians produce an unusual quantity of hot air. But lawmakers also produced a great deal of other detritus, as proved by the large number of ornate brass cuspidors supplied to the Capitol. Their presence suggests that lawmakers and state officials (all men at that time) expected to smoke cigars, chew tobacco, and spit at will throughout the new building. Bids for cuspidors were requested in 1912, and a contract was awarded to the lowest bidder: Keifer, Haessler Hardware Co. of Milwaukee. The heavy metal cuspidors—thirty-nine pounds of ornately decorated bronze with a steel liner—originally graced only the private offices of constitutional officers and legislators, but their popularity increased over the years. Perhaps they were seen as status symbols, since their number seems to have risen at the same pace that government grew.

By World War II, however, cuspidors began to be moved to storerooms. A 1955 inventory found 167 cuspidors in the state's possession, some of them still packed in their original crates. To the lawmakers of the fifties, the spittoons were just obsolete relics of the state's horse-and-buggy days. They were given away as souvenirs or sold for scrap metal, and they still show up

George B. Post & Sons created this blueprint of furniture details for the Capitol in 1910.

GEORGE B. POST & SONS #1991/146

One of the ornamented bronze cuspidors (or spittoons) designed by George B. Post & Sons

WHS MUSEUM #1955.3600

occasionally in Wisconsin antique shops having been converted into lamp bases or planters.

Porter usually had more important things on his mind than toilet seats and spittoons. But any minor part of the project could quickly transform into a political football that delayed progress or drove up costs. The petty egos of politicians gave him perpetual headaches.

For example, as spacious modern rooms opened up in the new wings, bureaucrats schemed to get better offices. The state fire marshal, the superintendent of public instruction, and the members of the Board of Immigration, the Railroad Commission, and the Highway Commission all lobbied Porter for larger quarters or nicer locations. By 1913, he was being deluged with demands, and he finally lost all patience when the state bank examiner deviated from the project plan while trying to secure a new space.

The bank examiner's office was scheduled to leave the old North Wing for modest offices in the new South Wing while its former quarters were demolished and new ones built. But the agency head wanted a much nicer temporary space and refused to leave, insisting that any new location had to have a bank vault.

Daniel Chester French's "Wisconsin" statue on top of the dome after regilding in 1990

WHI IMAGE ID 122057

This was not in the plans and would have caused delays, so Porter denied the examiner's request and ordered demolition of the old North Wing to start. But the bank examiner was just as stubborn and camped out in his old office while the North Wing came down around him. By mid-August 1913, most of it was merely a shell, and he still refused to accept his temporary accommodations.

After consulting the attorney general, Porter waited until his nemesis was briefly out of town and then ordered the corridor directly above the bank examiner's office to be dismantled. He scheduled the demolition to start after courts had closed for the day, in order to prevent a restraining order. As lathe and plaster began falling around the bank commissioner's staff, they quickly moved their furniture and files. And by the time the commissioner returned to Madison, his offices were gone.

Between 1904 and 1917, the years that the new capitol was under construction, the modern world as we know it was born. Airplanes, cars, radios, movies, electric appliances, paved roads, and birth control all became common for the first time. Einstein published his theory of relativity. Freud revealed that we don't usually act rationally. Oil was discovered in the Middle East. The NAACP began to fight for racial justice. Gertrude Stein, T. S. Eliot, James Joyce, and Virginia Woolf published their first books. W. C. Handy brought the blues to the American public. Stravinsky, Prokofiev, and Schoenberg invented modern classical music. Frank Lloyd Wright designed startling Prairie Style buildings. Picasso, Matisse, and Kandinsky produced the first modern art.

And the Capitol's designers wanted nothing to do with modernism.

Instead, at a time when every social, political, and artistic convention was being challenged, they chose to create a building that was nostalgic, reassuring, and safe. Its architecture mimicked ancient Greece, its sculptures echoed the Renaissance, and its paintings catered to Victorian trends from decades earlier. The Capitol's designers deliberately looked backward instead of forward. And they created a spectacular building that is still a stunning experience for thousands of visitors every year.

Architect George Post intended for the art that decorated the Capitol to be a positive force that would inspire and uplift its occupants, so he brought the best artists of the Gilded Age to Madison. Most had studied in New York, Boston, Paris, Rome, or Florence and had helped create other monumental public buildings, including the Library of Congress. Several had worked on state capitols in Massachusetts, Connecticut, Minnesota, Kentucky, Missouri, and Iowa. And some had worked on Post's lavish mansions or office buildings in New York.

Below: Model of the statue by Helen Farnsworth Mears that was rejected as "too heavy and bulky looking" for the top of the Capitol

WHI IMAGE ID 10588

Following pages: Capitol exterior photographed by James T. Potter

WHI IMAGE ID 44052

An exception was Helen Farnsworth Mears, a Wisconsin-born sculptor who had studied with Augustus Saint-Gaudens and designed a highly successful piece for the Columbian Exposition. In 1910, Mears was invited to create a statue to crown the top of the dome, the Capitol's single most important work. Although she was initially told she had won the contract after submitting three designs, Post and the Capitol Commission withdrew their invitation in 1911. Mears was paid for her time, but the lucrative contract went to Daniel Chester French.

Creating such an opulent capitol struck some lawmakers as wasteful and extravagant. Post's fee was calculated as a percentage of the total project cost, and Senator Spencer Marsh hinted that there was a direct relationship between the architect's specifications for expensive materials and his bank account. Marsh tried to prevent the state from spending enough money to realize Post's vision, but his proposal was rejected by the senate in a close vote.

Other Capitol officials objected not to the cost, but to the content of the art. The supreme court had always been decorated with portraits of past justices, and its current members, who looked forward to seeing their own portraits grace the courtroom, were incensed that artist Albert Herter had been commissioned to paint murals there instead. Post negotiated a compromise under which the entry room displayed portraits and the hearing room exhibited Herter's murals.

Painter Kenyon Cox offended Senator Henry Roethe by painting a nude sea nymph in a senate chamber mural. Roethe called this "a high degree inappropriate" and moved that the mural be taken down. His colleagues disagreed and his motion was defeated.

After the United States entered World War I in the spring of 1917, Senator M. W. Perry proposed that the German cross on the breast of a woman in another senate mural be covered with the American flag. His proposal passed and the mural was censored for the rest of the war.

More than five hundred contractors bid on 125 separate types of jobs (plumbing, painting, stonework, etc.), and for more than a decade, between twenty-five and forty of them were working simultaneously on any given day. It was the most complicated construction project ever attempted in the state, and Lew Porter was responsible for the success of every detail, from approving architectural drawings to inspecting paint on the moldings around doorways.

"As he walked about observing what was going on," recalled William Van Deusen, who watched the project daily from his father's store on South Carroll Street, "in his stoop-shouldered carriage of body and his slow but very cautious watching of what was going on, it seemed nothing escaped his eyes—that many workmen told me. That is, whatever the plan called for was carefully checked, and if the plan did not meet proper carrying out, that too was changed to fit."

The supreme court chamber, before restoration, with Albert Herter's mural, "The Signing of the American Constitution," in the background

WHI IMAGE ID 44014

Above: This senate
chamber triptych
features three paintings
by Kenyon Cox.

WHI IMAGE ID 44873

Right: Detail of
decorative molding

WHI IMAGE ID 45158

THE WISCONSIN CAPITOL

Once, when Porter suspected that an elaborate railing was not solid bronze as the specifications demanded, he got out a hacksaw and tore into it. He discovered that it was cast from a cheaper metal that had been plated in bronze and sent it back to be replaced. He personally designed the Capitol power plant six blocks away. This was connected to the Capitol by an eight-by-nine foot freight tunnel, and included living quarters for the engineer who was expected to be on call at any hour of the day or night.

Porter soothed the egos of pompous architects, butted heads with engineers, corralled striking stone masons, placated touchy artists, and outwitted conniving politicians. With an architect based in New York, contractors from Wisconsin and suppliers from the Midwest to Europe, Porter lived under intense stress for more than a decade. His every move was open to public scrutiny, and there was no escape. When he went home each night to Monona, the unfinished capitol haunted him from across the lake. When he took a rare day off to go sailing, his obligations loomed above him on the horizon.

Undated photograph of Lew Porter in a sailing canoe on Lake Mendota

The project took eleven years. Demolition of the charred ruins began in August 1906 when the burned out West Wing was tackled by the Madison firm of Polo Corona and Joe Oliva, who completed the tear-down in October. They then excavated the basement of the West Wing facing State Street, where the new capitol's first foundations were laid early in 1907. Wisconsin quarries couldn't provide light-colored granite for the exterior walls, so Porter took influential lawmakers on a tour of Georgia, Washington, DC, New York, and New England to inspect other public buildings and visit quarries. They settled on White Bethel granite from Woodbury Granite Co. of Hardwick, Vermont. In May 1907, Woodbury agreed to supply and install granite for the entire building for about $2,000,000. More luxurious materials were used on the interior: marble and other rare stone was shipped to Madison from six different US states and as far away as France, Italy, Greece, Germany, and Algeria.

Throughout the project, construction workers and state employees played musical chairs as portions of the old capitol came down and new ones went up:

1906: West Wing demolished.

1907: First foundation laid for the new West Wing.

1908: East Wing construction starts.

1909: Legislature meets for the first time in the
       new West Wing.

1910: East Wing construction ends and South Wing
       construction starts.

1911: Work on rotunda and dome starts.

1913: South Wing construction ends.

1914: North Wing construction starts. "Wisconsin"
       statue is installed atop the dome.

1915: Rotunda and dome construction ends. First public
       tours are given.

1917: North Wing construction ends.

The dome went up and the last fragments of the 1857–1869 building came down in 1913. The Capitol that we know today was finished in 1917 at a cost of $7,258,763.75, including removal of the ruins of the old capitol, construction of the heating plant six blocks away, and rent paid for office space after the 1904 fire. The Capitol Commission formally disbanded on July 1, 1917, but there was no celebration because the United States had just entered World War I, and Wisconsin residents were preparing to send their sons and brothers to fight on the battlefields of France.

Architect George Post didn't live to see his masterpiece completed. He died in 1913 while the dome was being erected, and his sons took over the project. Lew Porter literally worked himself to death, passing away at age fifty-six from hypertension and kidney disease just a few months after the building was finished. He's buried in Madison's Forest Hill Cemetery, where everyone who admires Wisconsin's capitol should pay a grateful visit.

Above: Work proceeds on the new capitol. The North Wing of the old capitol (right) remained in use until 1915.

WHI IMAGE ID 3482

Next page: Workers prepare to hoist the statue "Wisconsin" to the top of the Capitol dome.

WHI IMAGE ID 9566

5

Brave Men and Strong Women

In the early years of the new capitol, World War I dominated
life under the dome, as it did throughout the state and nation.
Wisconsin's National Guard was called out, and local draft boards
were set up in more than one hundred cities and towns throughout the state. Lawmakers created a state Council of Defense with
hundreds of county and local boards and committees to recruit
soldiers, grow food, encourage patriotism, and marshal supplies.
A state Woman's Committee enlisted thousands of women to
work on Americanization, child welfare, food production, and
nursing. Magnus Swensen, director of the Council of Defense,
originated "wheatless" and "meatless" days to conserve essential supplies and redirect them from the home front to soldiers.
State government threw itself wholeheartedly into the war effort.
Herbert Hoover quickly recognized the value of these measures
and implemented them on the national level.

On April 5, 1917, the night before the United States declared
war on the German Empire, President Woodrow Wilson told a

friend, "Once lead this people into war, and they'll forget there ever was such a thing as tolerance." He warned that under such circumstances, "conformity would be the only virtue, and every man who refused to conform would have to pay the penalty."

That was certainly true in Wisconsin, where seven hundred thousand immigrant and first-generation German American residents had no desire to make war on their relatives back home. At first, opposition to the war was widespread, and many state leaders spoke openly against American participation. Former Governor Robert La Follette, for example, blamed the war on "a comparatively few men in each government who saw in war an opportunity for profit and power for themselves." Before the war, Milwaukee socialists enjoyed electoral success, and during the war they denounced American participation as benefiting only "the Wall Street Clique that is behind Wilson and directs his actions." One journalist visiting Wisconsin in the summer of 1917 called it "really the most backward state I've struck in its sentiment toward the war." In the national press, Wisconsin was called "The Traitor State."

These charges emanated from critics who looked at Wisconsin and imagined traitors under every rock and behind every tree. In response, the state Council of Defense at the Capitol became an integral part of the machinery needed to organize and regiment society behind the war effort. Despite concerted action by Governor Emanuel Philipp to protect the civil liberties of Wisconsin residents, super patriots promoted the idea that anyone with ties to Germany or opinions critical of the war should be suspected of disloyalty. In Ashland, vigilantes tarred and feathered several people suspected of harboring German sympathies. In Clark County, a mob poured hundreds of bullets into the home of a German American family whose pacifist sons refused to register for the draft.

Everything German became suspect. In Wausau, the National German American Bank changed its name to the American National Bank. La Crosse banned the teaching of German in its

Sedition map created by the Wisconsin Loyalty League in 1918

WHI IMAGE ID 40882

elementary schools. Restaurants renamed sauerkraut "liberty cabbage," and wieners became "hotdogs." Milwaukee socialist Victor Berger was convicted of espionage (later overturned by the US Supreme Court) for publishing articles against the war. Milwaukee Germans expressed their frustration with wartime repression by electing Berger to Congress. Bob La Follette's political career was nearly ruined by attacks from his pro-war rivals.

Between 1914 and 1917, public opinion in Wisconsin gradually turned against Germany. Once war was formally declared, public opinion was overwhelmingly pro-war. Capitol officials were charged with implementing the federal Selective Service Act, and when Wisconsin men registered for the draft in June 1917, there were no significant protests. In the eighteen months of combat that followed, more than 122,000 soldiers from all around the state served in the military. Nearly four thousand lost their lives fighting for their country.

When the country entered World War I in the spring of 1917, women leaped into action by planting war gardens, knitting socks, raising money, selling Liberty Bonds, and becoming nurses. More than four hundred Wisconsin nurses served overseas with the Red Cross. As soon as the war ended, they mobilized against a bigger enemy, the Spanish Flu, which killed many more Americans than the war. Thanks in part to women's successful patriotic and medical work in 1917 and 1918, the US Senate approved a women's suffrage amendment on June 4, 1919.

It had been a long time coming. Bills that would have enabled women to vote in Wisconsin had been rejected in 1855 and 1867. A statewide referendum on the issue in 1912 was rejected two-to-one by the voters—all male, by definition. Bills to hold future referenda were repeatedly blocked at the Capitol, so Wisconsin women leaders focused their energy on Washington, DC, instead.

Anti-women's suffrage poster, ca. 1912

WHI IMAGE ID 1932

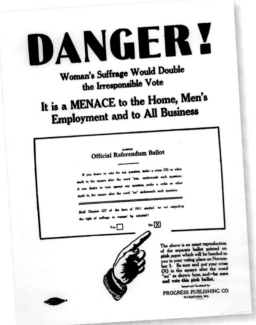

The day Congress approved the constitutional amendment, former First Lady Belle Case La Follette watched from the Congressional visitors' gallery and told her family that she "shed a few tears." Six days later, on June 10, Wisconsin became the first state in the nation to ratify the amendment (preceding Illinois by only a matter of hours). Robert La Follette proudly wrote to his family that Wisconsin "'beat 'em to it' on the suffrage amendment" because of "your smart mother."

The nineteenth amendment was finally ratified on August 18, 1920. The first Wisconsin woman to cast a ballot for president is thought to have been Ojibwe matriarch Flying Cloud, who voted in Odanah early on the morning of November 2, 1920. Another who voted that day was 106-year-old Louise Thiers of Milwaukee, whose father fought beside George Washington in the American Revolution. "I've waited a good many years for this opportunity," Thiers told reporters. "I can't tell you how glad I am." Besides voting for president, she also cast a ballot for one of the first female assembly candidates in Wisconsin, "for I believe if woman is qualified to vote she is qualified to hold office."

"The Nineteenth Amendment gave women the right to vote—period. Nothing more," wrote Mabel R. Putnam, president of the Wisconsin chapter of the National Women's League. She and thousands of other women still faced legal barriers in virtually all aspects of public life, from employment discrimination to property rights. But now that women could become a voting bloc, male politicians began to pay more attention to their concerns.

At the Capitol, Governor John J. Blaine endorsed an equal rights amendment when he ran for re-election in 1920. First Lady Anna Blaine was a good friend of Belle La Follette, and presumably both women encouraged its inclusion in the Republican Party platform. The amendment called for "equal pay for equal service regardless of sex" and demanded that "the legislature should revise our laws to the end that in all matters men and women should be upon a basis of equality."

Lawmakers introduced an equal rights bill in 1921 that would guarantee women "the same rights and privileges under the law as men in the exercise of suffrage, freedom of contract, choice of residence for voting purposes, jury service, holding office, holding and conveying property, care and custody of children and in all other respects." Blaine and La Follette lobbied women's groups across the state to pressure their lawmakers to support it.

But the very idea of women's equality frightened some legislators. One assemblyman argued, "This bill will result in coarsening the fiber of woman—it will take her out of her proper sphere." Another complained, "Why, a woman could establish her residence separate and apart from that of her husband, and continue to live away from him forever while he would have to support her

At an entrance to the Capitol, women congratulate Governor John Blaine for signing the Women's Rights Bill in 1921.

WHI IMAGE ID 118142

and could never divorce her." Proponents responded by threatening a roll call vote in which each lawmaker would have to go on record individually as opposing or supporting the measure. This raised the specter of women in every district organizing to defeat the bill's opponents in the next election, and arguments against the bill quickly evaporated.

The bill passed, and on July 11, 1921, Anna Blaine's husband signed the nation's first equal rights act into law. The National Women's Party called for celebration. "Under the laws of Wisconsin today," they announced, "women stand upon the same basis as men, freed from the ancient discriminations and disabilities which still fetter them in other states. Centuries of legal precedent and tradition, built upon the conception of women as inferior beings, and sanctioning with the majesty of the law the subjection of one-half of the race, have been overturned by Wisconsin with one clean stroke." Wisconsin women were soon taking civil service exams, serving on juries, renting their own homes, running for office, and handling their own business transactions. As they were challenged by adversaries, the law was repeatedly upheld by the Wisconsin Supreme Court.

Under the Capitol dome, however, lawmakers refused to obey the spirit of the law. A proviso in the bill preserved earlier labor laws protecting women workers from unusually long hours. Legislators claimed that governing was more than a nine-to-five job, refused to hire women, and laid off female staff, citing that provision.

This didn't keep women from running for state office, however. The first female legislators at the Capitol were three rural teachers elected to the assembly in 1924: Mildred Barber of Marathon County, Helen Brooks of Waushara County, and Helen Thompson of Price County. "The men didn't resent us too much," Barber recalled. Though, at that time, when Wisconsin was trying to avoid compliance with the Prohibition Act, some of the men disapproved of Brooks's support for the Women's Christian Temperance Union.

Mildred Barber, standing, and Helen Thompson and Helen Brooks, both sitting, in 1939

WHI IMAGE ID 65405

In 1929, Mary Kryszak of Milwaukee was elected to the senate and served almost continually until 1947. Described in the official state *Blue Book* as "a school teacher, music teacher, bookkeeper, librarian, and newspaper writer, as well as housewife and mother of three children," Kryszak also edited the newspaper *Glos Polek* (*Polish Women's Voice*) and was "active in many social, charitable, and political activities." For nearly all her tenure, she was the only woman lawmaker at the Capitol.

Female officeholders remained rare for decades to come. The first woman to hold a statewide constitutional office was Republican Glenn Wise, who was appointed secretary of state in 1955. Although she had a master's degree in economics and had worked in Washington, DC, she said she was "completely surprised" by the appointment and had to be persuaded to accept it. Wise was acting governor briefly in 1956, when the governor and lieutenant governor were both out of state. After losing the 1956 election, she shifted her focus to local politics in Madison.

Glenn Wise takes her oath of office, becoming the first woman to be sworn in for a state constitutional office.

The next year Dena Smith was appointed state treasurer. Her husband had been elected to the office for five consecutive terms starting in 1949, and she had worked as his administrative assistant. Although she lost in the next Republican primary, she was elected in 1960 without the backing of her own party, becoming the first woman elected to a statewide office. Smith served as treasurer until her death in 1968. Wisconsin voters would not fully embrace the idea of women legislators until the second wave of the women's movement in the 1970s.

By the 1920s, six hundred people worked in the Capitol every day and most of them weren't lawmakers. Legislators came to Madison for only a few months each year to sit in official sessions, but the rest of the time, civil servants hurried around the immense building trying to meet the needs of constituents. Custodian William Henwood literally held the key to their success or failure. Henwood was put in charge of Capitol security in 1900, and held that position through the fire, construction of the new building, and well into the Great Depression. He retired a few days before his death at age eighty in 1935.

"The Wisconsin Capitol is said to have the finest and at the same time the most intricate set of locks of any public building in America," reported the *Racine Journal-Times* in 1918. Each wing, office, desk, and mailbox had its own unique lock, so Henwood had to keep track of about six thousand keys. At first he kept them on a series of rings, but later he said: "I drew some plans and showed the governor how I could do the job better, and he let me have the vault built." The vault was a six-foot-square steel safe in which the keys were arranged on a series of hinged panels. Only Henwood possessed the master key that unlocked it.

He told the press in 1923 that while most Capitol workers appreciated the complexity of his job, one group was a particular thorn in his side. "I have more trouble with the state senators than with anyone else when it comes to lost keys," he said. "I'm always making a new set of keys for a senator to replace some that he has lost."

Visitors to the Capitol in 1920 hardly ever saw Henwood. To guests, the staff was personified by Stanley Lathrop and Albert Cook, the two official guides to the building. They gave seven tours a day to as many as one hundred thousand visitors a year, including foreign dignitaries, Madison school children, and love-struck honeymooners. Of the latter group, Lathrop said, "It is a waste of time for most of these people to go on the trip, for they never even see the building, much less hear what he has to say, so engrossed are they in each other."

Lathrop had fought in the Civil War before becoming an itin-erant minister and then a newspaper publisher. After retiring in 1914, he thought he'd enjoy showing people around the magnifi-cent new capitol and landed one of two jobs as tour leader. Cook, who joined him in 1917, was also a Civil War veteran. The two men wrote and published the first guide to the building, which quickly went through four editions. "Without a moment's hesita-tion," a reporter from Racine wrote in 1923, "they can tell you the date of some important event or what kind of marble is used in each corridor of the capitol."

Throughout the 1920s, jobs in the Capitol were used as a way to help elderly veterans. Before Social Security was introduced in 1935, many old people simply had to keep working if their family couldn't support them. In 1928, the Capitol staff included two aged Civil War veterans, Frank Higgins and Jesse Meyers.

Higgins had retired from his career as a rural school teacher in 1902 when one of his former pupils, Governor Robert La Follette, hired him to work as a clerk in the Capitol. For the next twenty-seven years he was in charge of all the office supplies issued to 1,700 state employees around Wisconsin. Higgins worked every day until his ninetieth birthday in 1929, and credited his long life to a youth of hard work on the family farm and always avoiding tobacco and alcohol.

Like Higgins, Jesse Meyers was a Civil War soldier who became a rural schoolteacher. He also spurned alcohol and even ran unsuccessfully for Congress on the Prohibition Party ticket in 1897. After retiring from a career in public service, Meyers was hired in 1901 to be assistant director of the Capitol's Grand Army of the Republic Museum (today's Wisconsin Veteran's Museum), and in 1924, at age eighty-one, he took over as its director. "I am still here at my desk putting in a regular day's work every day," he told a reporter in 1928.

That same year, Ho-Chunk elder Oliver La Mere was appointed a Capitol guide. He was born on the Nebraska Winnebago Reservation around 1870 into a prominent Winnebago family. On his mother's side, he was descended from the eighteenth-century female chief Glory-of-the-Morning. He was named for his paternal great grandfather, Oliver Armel, who lived beside the site of the future capitol during the 1830s. The Nebraska family kept in close touch with relatives in Wisconsin and often traveled back and forth.

As a child, La Mere was sent to the Indian Industrial School in Genoa, Nebraska, and the Carlisle Indian School in Pennsylvania, both of which tried to indoctrinate Native children with white values. La Mere managed to emerge from the boarding schools with his Ho-Chunk identity intact, as well as a deep understanding of white American culture. During his twenties, he became an important culture broker between the tribe and the outside world, serving as a translator, informant to anthropologists, and a contributor to academic works about the Ho-Chunk.

In 1915, La Mere began spending time in Wisconsin assisting anthropologists, lobbying for preservation of burial mounds, addressing community groups, and educating white audiences. "The Winnebagos were the first inhabitants of Wisconsin," he told a Madison group in 1927, "yet the people who live here now know nothing of their beautiful mythology, their age old traditions, their great moral truths founded on nature, their perfectly organized government."

To address this ignorance, La Mere brought an exhibit of cultural artifacts to the Capitol, where he formed a small museum on an upper floor under the dome. His collection included traditional

leather and woven clothes, beaded bags, carved bracelets and ear-
rings, a three-foot-long ceremonial pipe, and similar objects. The
state created a guide position for him, and he regularly provided
information to Boy Scouts, tourists, and other visitors interested in Wisconsin's earliest history. He held the job only briefly,
according to his friend, anthropologist Charles Brown, because
his educational work carried him far afield so often. "He goes all
over the United States on different missions," Brown said, "but
always comes back to Madison."

After his death on August 1, 1930, three trunks that held
La Mere's museum collection were given by his heirs to the
Wisconsin Historical Society, filled with dozens of artifacts
he'd carefully preserved during his decades of traveling. These

included two sacred peyote buds in a delicately beaded pouch, holy feathers, a large skin drum, a red stone pipe, and a ceremonial rattle used to help intrepid souls make their way along the peyote road in the depth of night.

One governor was actually adopted into the Ho-Chunk Nation during this era. On the night of August 23, 1927, beside the Wisconsin River, Governor Fred Zimmerman donned ceremonial clothes and joined in the tribe's traditional dancing and drumming to celebrate the occasion.

Zimmerman had been elected governor the previous year. His positions on the environment, historic preservation, and social justice had won the approval of many members of Wisconsin's Native American communities, including Oliver La Mere. Zimmerman's support for the recent efforts of La Mere and others to save ancient Ho-Chunk burial sites had impressed the tribe, and on August 16, 1927, they invited him to become an adopted tribal member.

The invitation and Zimmerman's acceptance reflected a shift in Indian-white relations during the 1920s. At this time, most Native American communities in Wisconsin were desperately poor. In 1887, the federal government had hoped to turn Indians into farmers by breaking tribal lands into small plots that were given to individuals tax-free for twenty years. But when the taxes came due around 1910, many native landowners were unable to pay and had to sell their land to white buyers, consequently becoming homeless. Their children were often taken away by government officials to boarding schools. They were given English names and forbidden to speak their own language. "They tried to erase us," one boarding school student recalled. Some children didn't see their families again until they were teenagers.

During the same years, Henry Ford began producing automobiles that middle-class Americans could afford, and tourism took on a new life. Wisconsin Dells, a traditional gathering place of the Ho-Chunk, became the center of Indian tourism after a white promoter, C. D. Parsons, staged pow-wows, dances, and other shows for customers arriving in Model Ts. Although his productions

commercialized Native culture for white entertainment, Parsons did provide much-needed income for the Indian actors and actresses. The Ho-Chunk adopted Parsons into their tribe as an expression of gratitude. However, white fantasies and Indian reality often clashed vividly. For example, in 1924, the city of Tomah organized a huge pageant celebrating the long-dead Menominee chief for whom the city was named, while just a few miles away, Indian children were being stripped of their culture in the Tomah Indian Industrial School.

Governor Zimmerman's adoption by the Ho-Chunk may have been a tourist stunt or a sincere appreciation for his interest in Indian causes. At the time, he was supporting preservation of ancient effigy mounds and a traditional Ho-Chunk village site at Frosts Woods, across Lake Monona from the Capitol. In a second ceremony there a few weeks later, the tribe named him a chief.

After taking part in the ceremony that summer night in the Dells, the governor was presented with a holy beaded pouch and a headdress. Zimmerman was humbled. "It makes me feel that I owe it to the Great Spirit to do all that I can for all my brethren," he replied. "May we, as Americans, all of us, leave this impressive ceremony with one purpose, to carry the spirit and the truth and the honesty of these people out into our state and into our country."

"The remainder of the evening was devoted to entertainment," a reporter noted, "of which the governor's dancing was not the least entertaining feature."

By the end of the 1920s, the Capitol was severely overcrowded. Wisconsin's population had grown to nearly three million people, and state offices expanded to meet increasing demands from residents. Progressive Republicans had passed laws regulating everything from child labor to food safety, which inspectors had to enforce. New technology played a role, too. For example, the invention of automobiles spawned an agency to issue drivers licenses, a State Highway Department to create safe roads, and an Oil Inspection Department to ensure reliable gasoline.

At the time, lawmakers worked in Madison for only a few months every other year; the rest of the time, the legislature was not in session. As soon as lawmakers left for their homes, the Capitol's full-time employees surged out of their cramped offices to take up residence in senate and assembly committee and caucus rooms, or even in the official chambers. When the next legislative session approached, they would pack up their files and cram their furniture back into their assigned spaces for a few months.

While this biennial juggling act was underway in December 1928, the *Capital Times* sent a reporter to investigate working conditions in the Capitol. "There is one well-known official using a women's lavatory for his office," William Dawson found, "while his stenographer occupies a bathroom just around the corner." Every basement corner, storage room, and corridor had been turned into office space. On the fourth floor, eighteen employees of one agency were crammed into a single room, and eleven staff of the Tax Commission worked in a blocked-off entryway. Temperatures reached 100 degrees in some places, ventilation and lighting were poor, and staff frequently became ill. "I am too sick to stand it longer," one clerk told coworkers as she resigned. "Life is too short."

These conditions prompted the construction of an office building two blocks away at 1 West Wilson Street, overlooking Lake Monona. The Highway Commission and Industrial Commission moved in when the building was completed in 1931. By that time, leaders in the Capitol had more important problems to deal with than crowded working conditions.

The stock market crash of October 1929 caused the worst depression in the nation's history. Wisconsin suffered terribly as factories closed, wages dropped, banks failed, farm values shrank, and unemployment swelled. So many Wisconsin banks failed that in March 1933, Governor Albert Schmedeman closed them all for two weeks to calm the volatile atmosphere. That same spring, dairy farmers in the Fox River Valley went on strike, withholding milk, closing down cheese factories, and barricading roads in a vain attempt to raise market prices.

Everyone thought they knew who was to blame and what should be done. In Milwaukee, strikes increased sevenfold between 1933 and 1934. Violence broke out in rural counties as farmers sought to halt the delivery of milk until they received better prices. People lost their jobs all across the state. And without any temporary help from the government, the unemployed were forced to fend for themselves. That is, until Wisconsin officials crafted the country's first unemployment compensation law.

The idea had been proposed in 1918, but no one had wanted to pay for it then. Businesses said they couldn't afford it, conservatives said government shouldn't intervene in such private affairs, and radicals said it should intervene more. But as the Depression put hundreds of thousands of Wisconsinites out of work, Governor Philip (Phil) La Follette—Fighting Bob's son, who served as governor for most of the 1930s—forged a compromise. Communist agitators and corporate bankers, Milwaukee socialists and Fox Valley mill owners, rural farmers and urban unions, Progressives and Republicans all gradually lined up

A view of the state
office building in 1941

behind the same proposal, and Wisconsin's unemployment compensation act was passed on January 28, 1932.

Under the law, employers voluntarily contributed no more than 2 percent of their payroll to an insurance fund. If enough businesses failed to pitch in, contributions became mandatory, but if a business hired enough workers it contributed even less than 2 percent. Workers who'd lost jobs could collect 50 percent of their wages (not to exceed $10 per week) for not more than thirteen weeks. The law ignored workers in many industries and those who had worked fewer than forty total weeks in Wisconsin.

Although officials expected the insurance fund to grow large enough in eighteen months to support claimants, the economy withered and many businesses couldn't contribute anything at all. The state's first unemployment check was not issued until August 17, 1936, to Neils Ruud of Madison. By then, the federal government had made unemployment compensation a federal law.

President Franklin Roosevelt had asked Wisconsin economists Arthur Altmeyer and Edwin Witte to come up with a national

THE WISCONSIN CAPITOL

program similar to Wisconsin's that would protect the unemployed, the elderly, the disabled, and others who could not work. They drafted the Social Security Act, which Congress passed in 1935. Since then, it has provided a safety net for millions of hardworking Americans suffering from the effects of economic forces beyond their control.

During the years of the Great Depression, as businesses closed and citizens lost their jobs, fewer tax dollars flowed into the Capitol. State officials had to cut back on spending and stretch every dollar, but thousands of residents also desperately needed help. State treasurer Sol Levitan was charged with solving this dilemma. He was later remembered as one of Wisconsin's most flamboyant and best-loved politicians.

Levitan was born into a poor Jewish family in Tilsit, East Prussia, in 1862. When he rescued his employer's family from an anti-Semitic mob in 1880, his grateful boss offered to pay for either a university education or a ticket to America. Levitan took the ticket. He arrived in the United States penniless and unable to speak a word of English but inspired by the American dream.

He worked as an itinerant peddler, selling clothes and housewares from a backpack. In 1881, he found loyal customers in the German and Swiss areas of Dane and Green Counties, including a young lawyer named Robert La Follette. Levitan sold him a pair of suspenders and became a lifelong friend and supporter.

In 1887, Levitan opened a store in New Glarus that soon sprouted successful branches in neighboring towns, enabling him to start a bank. This flourished, too, and in 1905 he moved to Madison to take over the Commercial National Bank. When its directors were reluctant to name a Jew as president, Levitan showed them his stock certificates and pointed out, "I own the bank." That settled the issue.

As a young traveling salesman, Levitan had been laughed at by a banker in Monroe who told him that a "Jew peddler" would never amount to anything. One of his first acts as bank president was to mail a note to the man, reminding him of his erroneous prediction. Unfortunately, Levitan faced blatant anti-Semitism throughout his career. Wisconsin's Jewish communities were tiny, and the racist, anti-immigrant Ku Klux Klan had as many as 75,000 Wisconsin members during the 1920s.

Despite the hostile environment, Levitan threw himself into politics. "When I moved to Madison," he said later, "La Follette and I were neighbors. And he always said that people were not getting fair play and something should be done to change conditions." He discovered that his foreign accent, his broken English, and his stereotypical mannerisms could be an asset if he played them to his advantage. At one debate, an opponent for state treasurer made a clearly anti-Semitic speech stressing the "stinginess" of Jews. Levitan responded that he tended to agree: "Elect me, a stingy man, as your State Treasurer, and I won't squander any of your money." He won, and served as state treasurer for nearly all of the 1920s and 1930s.

Levitan had an innate marketing instinct and a boundless appetite for publicity. Due to his door-to-door sales in the 1880s and his banking contacts in the 1890s, he was known to thousands of Wisconsin residents as "Uncle Sol." It was said that he never foreclosed on a mortgage and never refused to cash a farmer's check. In his first term as treasurer, he modernized accounting practices, collected millions in back taxes, streamlined red tape, and distributed the state's money into small-town banks rather than centralizing it in Madison.

Treasurer Levitan was re-elected again and again, sometimes garnering more votes than the governor. As he grew old, outsiders criticized him for continuing to run. "It might be good to let an elderly man handle your money," he replied. "He's looking for the golden gate, not the golden calf." Levitan passed through that gate on February 27, 1940, beloved by thousands.

In the upheaval caused by the Depression, Wisconsin politics in the 1930s became divided into more factions than ever before. Conservative Republicans, who had faith that the private sector could lift the nation out of the Depression, continued to wrestle

with Progressive Republicans for control of the party. Much to everyone's surprise, in 1932, the Democrats, who'd been hibernating for forty years, rode into office on the coattails of Franklin Roosevelt and his promise of government intervention in the economy. By 1934, the Progressive Republicans had decided that FDR's New Deal was not bold enough and formed their own new organization, the Progressive Party of Wisconsin, in alliance with labor unions. Meanwhile, in Milwaukee, Socialists continued to run the city government and send their party's representatives to Madison.

These four factions—Republican, Democrat, Progressive, and Socialist—debated, fought, and occasionally compromised under the Capitol dome throughout the Depression years. Businessmen, union bosses, Marxist ideologues, and New Deal liberals took turns blaming each other for society's problems and trying to impose their own solutions.

State Treasurer Sol Levitan sits surrounded by his employees in the state treasurer's office as they celebrate his victory in the primary election in 1930.

WHI IMAGE ID 20066

Each had its partisan mouthpieces in the media, too, as newspapers and even specific reporters defended different viewpoints. Lawmakers moved from one party to another as political events unfolded in Madison and Washington, and it seemed at times as if Wisconsin residents would need a scorecard to keep track of the shifting alliances. Personal popularity counted as much as party loyalty for many voters. Phil La Follette was elected governor for most of the decade—in 1930 as a Republican, and in 1934 and 1936 as a Progressive—as a result of his famous name as much as his harmony with voters' political views.

During Phil La Follette's first term as governor, the Conservation Commission made a stink at the Capitol. "One of the greatest obstacles to jurisprudence ever encountered by the Wisconsin Supreme Court was removed today," wrote the *Sheboygan Press* on Wednesday, October 19, 1932. "It was a dead fish in a vault below the court chambers."

For years, state conservation statutes required that confiscated fish and game had to be sold for the state's benefit. Game wardens enforcing the law in rural areas, however, were sometimes lax about complying. In 1932, rumors reached the Capitol that these wardens sometimes personally ate or sold animals seized in the line of duty. So Madison authorities decided to hold wardens accountable for the proper disposal of confiscated game, and a new provision was inserted in the legal code requiring that seized fish and game be sent to the Capitol.

A captured sturgeon was soon deposited, unpreserved, in a basement storage room next to an elevator shaft that rose up beside the supreme court chambers. A large piece of venison soon joined it. As bacteria began to work their magic on the abandoned flesh, unintended consequences of the new regulation began to waft into powerful noses.

Ever dignified, members of the supreme court initially tried to ignore the stench rising up the elevator

1938 Political poster

WHI IMAGE ID 96946

Governor Philip
La Follette at his desk
in the Capitol, ca. 1931

WHI IMAGE ID 121139

shaft. But as odors intensified, the justices decided that laws about abating a public nuisance trumped those about confiscated game. Elevator operators were less judicial: "If it had been a private institution," one of them complained, "there would have been 96 inspectors in here."

Capitol custodian Tony Pickarts was instructed to remove the nuisance. This was a risky decision, because Pickarts had almost shut down state government two years before when he tried to skin a skunk on the Capitol grounds. "I want it distinctly understood," he argued in his own defense, "that I was not to blame then. That skunk had been run over by an automobile. I merely stuck a knife into it—and you know what happened."

He had better luck with the rotting sturgeon. Pickarts's investigation led him to the Conservation Commission's basement storeroom. After removing the decaying venison and sturgeon, he was still faced with the problem of a lingering stench rising from the floor. It took state-of-the-art disinfectants to finally wipe out all vestiges of the dead animals.

Group portrait of eight Capitol "scrubwomen" in 1933

WHI IMAGE ID 17258

Some Capitol dignitaries were said to be so scarred by the experience that they swore off sturgeon altogether, even caviar. The provision was revoked and conservation wardens were once again entrusted with disposing of confiscated game locally, which probably helped them and their neighbors cope with the desperate rural poverty brought on by the Great Depression.

Despite the shadow that the Great Depression cast over the state in the 1930s, some newspapers still had a sense of humor. On a lovely spring morning in 1933, residents around the state woke up to a terrifying headline: "Extra! Explosions Blow Dome Off State Capitol!" Their shock quickly turned to laughter as they read on: "Officials Say Legislature Generated Too Much Hot Air."

It was April Fool's Day:

Wisconsin's beautiful $8,000,000 capitol building was in ruins today, following a series of mysterious explosions which blasted the majestic dome from its base and sent it crashing through the roof of the East Wing.

At 7:30 this morning the first mighty explosion occurred, rocking the dome and shattering windows throughout the city. This was followed immediately by two lesser blasts which sent showers of granite chips down upon the heads of pedestrians. . . .

Authorities were considering the possibility that large amounts of gas, generated through many weeks of verbose debate in the senate and assembly chambers, had in some way been ignited, causing the first blast.

It is believed the other five blasts were indirectly caused by the first, which set off excess quantities of hot air that had seeped from the assembly and senate chambers in to other rooms in the building.

But getting by during the Great Depression was no joke. Even employees of the federal Works Projects Administration struggled to make a living wage. WPA jobs paid only a fraction of what private businesses paid for the same work. Because Washington officials

Image printed under the headline "Extra! Explosions Blow Dome Off State Capitol!"

CAPITAL TIMES, APRIL 1, 1933

were constantly shifting funds from one state to another and cutting the agency's budget on short notice, Wisconsin administrators couldn't always guarantee a full week's pay. Most WPA employees found that they simply could not keep body and soul together.

So on March 10, 1936, federal workers in Oshkosh, Fond du Lac, Sheboygan, and Green Bay threatened to strike. When they were ignored, they came to Madison to meet with the WPA director. After being told that he was out of town, one striker replied, "If he is, he sneaked out when he heard we was coming." So the workers took over the assembly chamber in the Capitol and vowed to stay until their demands were met. Many brought their families, and eventually 184 protesters were camped out under the dome. They found local support among Madison residents. Grocers provided discounted food. At one point, Governor Phil La Follette gave them $30 out of his own pocket.

State lawmakers were adjourned at the time, so the protesters held a mock session of their own with comic bills and sarcastic resolutions. But their intentions were entirely serious. "Next time the legislators convene, we will be down here with clubs and make them come across with workers' demands," announced one of their leaders. "Bull won't go anymore, because we'll have pick axes to hold over them."

Unfortunately, WPA wages and working conditions were a federal matter rather than a state one. Wisconsin lawmakers had no power to solve the strikers' problems. When seventy Madison police officers came to evict them, strike leader Lyle Olson announced, "We came down without violence, and we'll leave without violence." After ten days they departed peacefully, with none of their demands met.

Just a few months after the strike, on May 15, 1936, the Capitol's flags flew at half-mast for one of the most popular men to work within its walls. The person buried that day was not a governor, or senate president, or chief justice of the supreme court, or famous general, or statesman, but Samuel Pierce—receptionist for five governors and friend to all who knew him.

Pierce was born in 1870 in New Orleans to parents who spent their early lives enslaved. "No one in my family was ever sold," his mother said. "They wouldn't ever part with us because we did our work so good." The Pierce family moved to Louisiana, where Sam's father was a judge and legislator until the rise of Jim Crow laws and the Ku Klux Klan effectively barred African Americans from positions of authority.

In about 1888, young Sam Pierce landed a job as a Pullman porter, a servant on long-distance railroad trips, which was one of the few good jobs open to people of color in segregated America. He learned how to speak and act in ways that pleased affluent white passengers and traveled beyond the Deep South. In 1905, he was assigned to the Chicago-Minneapolis route, which brought him in daily contact with government officials commuting between Milwaukee and Madison. One of them recalled Pierce as "definitely an optimist and a philosopher who made the best of things. His smile was contagious, his courtesy and diplomacy unfailing." Pierce settled his family, including his elderly mother, in Madison in 1907, and in 1922, Governor John Blaine asked if Pierce would serve as receptionist in the executive office.

In this new position, Pierce was essentially Blaine's gate-keeper. Lobbyists, reporters, civil servants, constituents, businessmen, tourists, and self-promoters of all kinds wanted access to the governor. His job was to keep them away.

Standing more than six feet tall and always dressed impeccably in a blue suit, Pierce gently defended the executive office from intruders. One visitor wrote that "Sam greeted every caller with a warm, cheery smile and a never failing observation that it was 'a nice day, suh.' It mattered not one bit that it might be a dreary day outdoors, cloudy and slushy, for to Sam it was always a nice day." Pierce's years of experience navigating white people's moods on railroad cars had prepared him for the Capitol. "He had a genius for avoiding offense," a visiting US State Department official remarked. "I called there three times, went in the front door, Sam

Samuel Pierce at
a desk in the executive
offices of the governor,
ca. 1930

WHI IMAGE ID 37461

and I talked, and as we were talking we moved about. Sooner or later, I found myself going out of the entrance. He wasn't trying to get me into the governor's office, he was just quietly oozing me out of the place."

Pierce fulfilled the expectations of white dignitaries about how a black servant should behave, and his flawless etiquette and Southern charm always reassured them. But no one ever got in to see the governor unless he said so. "A gentle pat," recalled a Capitol reporter, "a whisk of his hand at an imaginary fleck of dust, sent many of them away in a congenial mood, even if they had failed to see the governor himself and were forced to conduct their affairs with some minor official."

A few blocks away in Madison's African American neighborhood, Pierce "was really a power himself in his community," a Madison acquaintance recalled. "He was unofficially a judge and arbiter for his people and worked ceaselessly to prevent disputes. Time after time Negro neighbors brought their quarrels to Sam, and invariably they left satisfied with his simple but honest justice." After witnessing discrimination against visiting black entertainers by Madison hotel owners, he lobbied for fair accommodations. In the 1930s, he urged the creation of a cultural center in the black community where reading, discussion groups, classes, concerts, plays, and other activities could take place.

Pierce died at age sixty-six after a brief illness. Governor Phil La Follette visited him in the hospital, and when Pierce died unexpectedly following surgery, five different governors paid tribute to him in the press and obituaries appeared in newspapers all across the state. "His solicitous courtesy and unfailing smile endeared him to co-workers and thousands of capitol visitors," wrote a La Crosse reporter. "He did a great deal of good, and made a great many friends," another wrote. "How much more can a governor do, or a president, or the ruler of the world's greatest empire?"

State agencies expanded in size and number during the 1930s as they tried to relieve hardship caused by the Depression and stimulate the economy. In Madison, state employees were again working in cramped quarters or rented office space around the Capitol Square. In 1935, Governor Phil La Follette introduced a budget that included funds for a second state office building on West Wilson Street, right next to the one constructed in 1931.

"Under the detailed program which the legislature will be asked to approve," the press reported, "the state will construct a new office building adjoining the Monona Ave. Capitol Annex at a cost of $1,180,000. . . . The new state office building would be 11 stories high and would be designed to house all state departments now leasing quarters in private buildings. An official estimate showed that the state now pays rent for 66,600 net square feet of office and laboratory space."

Battles followed in the legislature over whether new government offices in Madison were a proper expense when thousands of rural citizens were living in great poverty. They also argued over who would pay for the new office building and who would oversee construction. After three years of haggling, the project was financed with 55 percent state funds and 45 percent federal funds, and construction began in the fall of 1938. Prisoners were released from their cells to quarry granite in northeastern Wisconsin (an idea that sparked much debate), workers went on strike for higher wages, and union workers walked off the job over who would get which contracts, but after eighteen months the building was ready.

The roster of agencies that left the Capitol provides a snapshot of how much government had grown. Tenants of the new building on July 1, 1940, included the Motor Vehicle Department, Board of Health, Public Service Commission, Department of Taxation, Industrial Commission, Planning Board, Highway Commission, Conservation Department, Real Estate Board, Painters' License Division, Gas Inspection Division, and Board of Deposits. As decades rolled by, a third and final wing of the annex opened in 1959, which was quickly followed by the Hill Farms State Office building on Madison's west side in 1964.

In the summer of 1940, Capitol officials breathed a sigh of relief and workers played musical chairs. As they moved into newly vacated offices, they trampled on the Capitol designers' original intentions for how rooms should be used. Conspicuous ceremonial spaces like the rotunda, governor's office, supreme court, and senate and assembly chambers were left largely intact,

Office workers process birth certificates in the Wisconsin State Office Building on West Wilson Street in 1942.

WHI IMAGE ID 13864

THE WISCONSIN CAPITOL

but staff offices were subdivided, retrofitted, partitioned off, and redecorated.

Managers tossed out old oak roll-top desks in favor of modern grey steel, and other original furnishings met similar fates. Of the roughly 3,500 pieces of furniture created for the Capitol a century ago, only about 1,000 survive today. Walls were painted drab green, richly woven carpets were replaced with cheap synthetics, and suspended panels with fluorescent lights were hung from ceilings. Original marble, plaster, granite, and carved wooden features were knocked down or covered over. A few well-intentioned amateurs did more harm than good as they touched up the original paintings and mosaics. By mid-century, the once-luxurious interior looked worn out and shabby. "Eventually," wrote Capitol historian Michael Keane, "most Capitol workers would forget that there had ever been a unified decorative scheme for the interior rooms."

Today, the assembly parlor is trimmed in Circassian walnut paneling with mantels of Sienna yellow marble and a marble tile floor.

WHI IMAGE ID 45090

In Our Times

World War II finally put an end to the Great Depression. The economic machine that had collapsed in 1929 came back to life as the federal government prepared for war. Orders for guns, trucks, ships, planes, and a thousand other necessities set factories humming again. Workers who'd been living on welfare or unemployment checks streamed into well-paying, reliable jobs. Men enlisted in the military and women took jobs on assembly lines. But business at the Capitol didn't exactly proceed as usual.

In November 1942, for example, Spike Loomis of Mauston won the gubernatorial election by a landslide but never took office. Loomis was a small-town kid who made it to college, fought in World War I, attended law school, and was elected city attorney and then state attorney general. As a Progressive, he refused to enforce Prohibition laws in the 1920s, and he designed the state's rural electrification program in the 1930s. Enabling power, light, and alcohol to flow through the state endeared him to voters, and he trounced incumbent Milwaukee millionaire Julius Heil in the 1942 election. Then, before he could take office, Loomis died from a sudden heart attack at age forty-nine.

The state constitution didn't address this predicament. It stated that the lieutenant governor would step in if a governor passed away in office, but Loomis had never taken office. There was an incumbent lieutenant governor, but he had just been rejected by voters alongside Heil. The incoming lieutenant governor, Walter Goodland, was not even in the same party as Loomis, and voters had never endorsed him for the state's top office. Heil's supporters argued that he should be retained as governor at least until a special election could be held, or that he should be allowed to appoint the next governor. Everyone under the Capitol dome and in the media had his or her own opinion about what should be done.

They all agreed, however, that the proper arbiter of the situation should be the Wisconsin Supreme Court. After reviewing the 1847–1848 constitutional debates and the 1855 dilemma of two candidates claiming simultaneous victories, the court decided that the incoming lieutenant governor who voters had chosen should become the state's next chief executive. Eighty-year-old Republican Walter Goodland of Racine took Loomis's place on inauguration day.

Goodland became a sort of unifying father figure, or maybe grandfather figure, as the state grappled with World War II, and voters re-elected him in 1944 and 1946. He was a bit of a renegade in his own party, and its political in-fighting subsided during his administration. The Progressive Party of the La Follette family was defeated in statewide contests and eventually disbanded in 1948. Socialists returned to focusing on Milwaukee, and Democrats returned to obscurity. The Capitol would remain securely Republican throughout the 1940s and most of the 1950s.

The booming private sector and recruitment efforts during the war years also disrupted

Loomis campaign poster, ca. 1941

WHI IMAGE ID 91450

life at the Capitol. Male staff departed for the front, including clerks, bureaucrats, and even high-ranking officials such as former Governor Phil La Follette, who served in the Pacific with General Douglas MacArthur. The turnover in the Capitol workforce prompted lawmakers to hire a consulting firm to survey and analyze the state's personnel system in September 1946. Griffenhagen and Associates of Chicago spent seven months examining Wisconsin's state agencies and comparing them to businesses in the private sector.

Then, as now, many citizens outside Madison regarded state workers with a certain resentment and disdain. Much of it was based on stereotypes of Roosevelt's 1930s public works programs, especially the Works Progress Administration, whose initials were popularly said to stand for "we poke around" or "whistle, piss, and argue." In 1932, when political appointees illegally displaced Wisconsin's state workers, the government workers had unionized and the union's widely publicized victory only reinforced the notion that Capitol workers had cushy jobs with privileges denied to others.

The Griffenhagen survey discovered, however, that the stereotype was largely unfounded. It was true that state workers in low-paying, subordinate jobs often earned more than their peers in private business. But civil servants in professional positions generally received compensation equal to people doing similar work in the private sector, and supervisors and managers working for the state were paid considerably less than their counterparts in corporations. As for fringe benefits, Capitol employees were found to have more vacation time, more sick leave, and more paid holidays than their peers, but workers in the private sector had shorter hours, more opportunity to earn overtime, better insurance packages, more frequent raises, and better chances at promotion.

"The great majority of state workers," wrote a conservative *Wisconsin State Journal* reporter after reading the report, "are hard-working, serious men and women who give their best to their jobs." But he endorsed the report's recommendation that raises based on seniority should be replaced by true merit raises based on performance and that inefficiencies uncovered in certain departments should be eliminated.

On April 16, 1947, lawmakers pondering the Griffenhagen report encountered some real monkey business at the Capitol when an African monkey owned by a returning GI appeared before the assembly's committee on municipalities. The GI, David Mackin, had won the monkey, Joe, in a dice game with French sailors in North Africa during the war. Joe was embraced by Mackin's unit much as Old Abe the eagle had been adopted by Wisconsin's Eighth Infantry during the Civil War. When the war ended, Mackin took the tame monkey home with him to Milwaukee as a pet.

Joe behaved as curious monkeys will and sometimes terrorized the neighborhood. When residents complained, Mackin blamed the humans, insisting they'd teased and baited Joe. When people tried to take him to court, they found there was no county ordinance or state statute concerning monkeys, so they had one introduced in the assembly.

On April 16, 1947, the aggrieved neighbors, David Mackin, legislators, aides, and Joe the monkey all crowded into a hearing room at the Capitol to testify about Assembly Bill 434. The draft bill revised a statute originally intended to curb rabid dogs, replacing the word "dogs" with "animals": "Any person may kill any animal . . . that may suddenly assault him while he is peacefully walking or riding and while being out of the inclosure [*sic*] of its owner."

Six neighbors testified that Joe was a dangerous nuisance. One described how her daughter had been bitten by the monkey; another explained how Joe frightened her children. Mackin responded that the children had abused and taunted Joe, and according to one reporter, the hearing quickly descended into "he-said-she-said acrimony while Joe the monkey sat placidly in Mackin's arms observing how the human primates behaved."

When the proposed text of the law was reviewed, the legislator for the neighbors and the lobbyist for Milwaukee County both supported it. Mackin concluded his opposition by stating, "It's all right if you treat my monkey like other pets but I don't want anyone coming into my yard and killing him." An attorney in the room emphasized that the neighbors already had the right to sue for damages if they felt aggrieved and, after pointing out that humans are also animals, cautioned that the new law was "so broad that one man might be able to chase another man into his own yard and shoot him on the grounds that he was vicious." After the hearing, when everyone went back to Milwaukee, it was decided that animal control was a matter for local governments to legislate rather than the state.

THE WISCONSIN CAPITOL

While Assembly Bill 434 died a quiet death, other movements in the Capitol were just coming to life. In the late 1940s, a group of young liberals decided to reinvent the state's Democratic Party.

It was a crazy idea because Wisconsin had drifted to the right during World War II. Republicans had firm control of the Capitol, Socialists had retreated to Milwaukee before finally admitting defeat, and the Progressive Party had disbanded in 1946. "They were gone," recalled Democratic strategist Bill Cherkasky. "And the Democratic Party didn't exist, really. Even though there was a Democratic President—Harry Truman—there was no Democratic Party in Wisconsin."

That left a vacuum for a handful of idealists to fill. Ellen Proxmire recalled, "It was like a cell, almost, because these were all people who were interested in the cause, but there was no office, there was no formal organization, certainly no money." Women were crucial to the success of the new movement. "We all loved it," Proxmire continued. "We socialized together. We all knew each other. We all knew our children. . . . There was a small office over on the Square in Madison on Mifflin Street. We had this small, crummy office over a bakery, I think, and [Fran Letcher] and I were the two paid employees for the Democratic—it was called The Democratic Organizing Committee then."

Its leaders were young World War II vets who believed in both free enterprise and a strong government that looked out for common people. Future governors Gaylord Nelson, Patrick Lucey, and John Reynolds launched their careers from this fringe group, as did future senator William "Bill" Proxmire. "These were fresh new faces," said Cherkasky, "young people, very attractive, good looking, with progressive values. They were not way out in left field somewhere. They campaigned hard. And I think people grew to like them."

In fact, voters liked them so much that by 1950 there were thirty-two Democratic lawmakers sitting under the Capitol dome, and the party was ready to run viable candidates for statewide and national offices.

Two notable leaders of this new party were Gaylord Nelson and Bill Proxmire, friends who could hardly have been more different. Nelson was an intellectual and introvert who always had a tall stack of half-finished books on his nightstand. But he'd grown up in the small northern town of Clear Lake and understood the needs and values of his constituents. Proxmire was a born extrovert who became legendary for shaking hands outside Packers games, state fairs, and factory gates in order to meet voters one-on-one. But he was also a stubborn maverick who sometimes struggled to empathize with his constituents. Both men served the state for decades in Washington, but Nelson cut his teeth under the Capitol dome.

Before coming to Madison, Nelson had spent long hours on a World War II troop ship reading books about wildlife and the environment. When he entered politics in 1948, he knew that conservation would be one of his main priorities. The state had created a Conservation Commission in 1927, but under Republican control it focused largely on the interests of lumber and paper companies. The commission was advised by a coterie of academics, corporate executives, and groups of outdoorsmen

Senators Gaylord
Nelson and William
Proxmire

WHI IMAGE ID 30135

THE WISCONSIN CAPITOL

that Nelson called "nothing more than a rich man's rod and gun club." He was one of the few politicians at the Capitol concerned by wider environmental issues.

During the mid-1950s, Republican control of the state began to wobble, undermined partly by the embarrassment of Senator Joe McCarthy's excessive anti-communism and partly by an economic downturn. In 1958, after Proxmire had lost several governor's races, the Democrats ran Nelson. He traveled to small towns in seventy counties that fall, logging more than thirty thousand miles and shaking hands Proxmire-style everywhere he went. In November, he unseated the incumbent Republican, inspiring enough Democratic voters to also capture the assembly and four out of five statewide offices. History had repeated itself: the fledgling Democrats had stormed the Capitol like the upstart Republicans had done a century earlier.

Governor Nelson went on to establish Wisconsin as a national leader in environmental issues by creating the pioneering

A view of the Capitol from the intersection of State and West Johnson Streets, ca. 1957

WHI IMAGE ID 119126

Outdoor Recreation Acquisition Program. Passed in 1961, it pledged $50 million over the next decade toward environmental planning, acquisition of land for preservation, and easements along state highways to ensure scenic views. After his election to the US Senate in 1962, Nelson was instrumental in creating the Environmental Protection Agency, outlawing the pesticide DDT, helping to pass the clean air and water acts, and creating the Apostle Islands National Lakeshore. In 1970, he established Earth Day, which may have done more to raise the environmental consciousness of the country than any other single act.

While the sixties were important years for the environmental movement, the decade is also remembered for its protests, and the Capitol was an obvious focal point for anyone with an axe to grind. As a landmark and a symbol, as well as the workplace of Wisconsin lawmakers, it was the first place activists chose to assemble when voicing their anger, frustrations, and hopes. And no issue provoked as many dramatic Capitol protests as the war in Vietnam.

For example, on Saturday, October 16, 1965, demonstrators gathered for the second day of the International Days of Protest. The Madison-based National Coordinating Committee to End the War in Vietnam had helped coordinate rallies across the country. The first day's activities that Friday had included teach-ins on the UW–Madison campus, and on Saturday hundreds of protesters marched up State Street to listen to speakers on the Capitol Square. At one point, a group headed for Truax Field in an attempt to make a citizens' arrest of the base commander. They formed a human barricade in front of the entrance to the Madison military base, where several were arrested.

Antiwar protests continued at the Capitol that fall, and demonstrators were often challenged by those who supported the war. On several occasions, veterans from local VFW and American Legion posts outnumbered the protesters. Though mostly peaceful, these confrontations occasionally erupted into minor violence, as when antiwar protesters were pelted with eggs at the

Capitol in November 1965. They were just the first engagements in a home front struggle that would grow increasingly bitter, divisive, and painful over the next decade.

Five years later, on April 18, 1970, the Madison Area Peace Action Council joined the Veterans for Peace in Vietnam in a march for peace at the Capitol. About eight thousand people showed up to voice their hope for a peaceful end to the war. Trailing them, a group of four hundred "revolutionaries" (in the words of the media) marched to the Capitol flanked by Madison police dressed in riot gear. Their chants praising Ho Chi Minh were answered by "Peace, Now" from the larger crowd.

Midway through the planned speeches, this band of revolutionaries left, shouting "Victory for the Viet Cong" and smashing shop windows on State Street. After the police tried to halt the rampage, hundreds of people filled the downtown area, destroying

A large crowd demonstrates against the war in Vietnam, as seen from the steps of the Capitol looking down State Street, ca. 1970.

WHI IMAGE ID 67628

property and overturning cars while police fired smoke bombs and charged into crowds with their nightsticks. It was neither the first nor the last riot near the Capitol that summer, a trend that culminated on August 24 with the bombing of Sterling Hall (where military research was being done) on the UW campus, which killed an innocent bystander.

Saigon's fall to the North Vietnamese Army on April 30, 1975, ended the protests as well as the war. A crowd of four hundred gathered at the Capitol that night to observe the final act in the conflict. Many shared the sentiments of one city worker who said, simply: "There's nothing to celebrate, but I'm glad we're out."

Since its construction, the Capitol has hosted countless rallies and protests, some planned and others spontaneous, some permitted and others illegal, as the people of Wisconsin have used the state's most cherished landmark to highlight their causes. One of the most dramatic protests at the Capitol happened on September 29, 1969, as the legislature was about to convene a special budget session that included possible cuts to welfare.

Milwaukee civil rights leader Father James Groppi, who had helped organize the city's desegregation movement, had led dozens of poor black and Hispanic families on a week-long march to Madison. In some small towns, residents heckled the marchers and shops barred their doors, but in others, farmers provided food and places for them to sleep. When they reached Madison on Sunday, September 28, one thousand supporters gathered to listen to the protesters describe their lives and condemn "a country that places so much emphasis on the military and cannot feed its own children," in Father Groppi's words. Referring to the legislature's budget, he said, "We're tired of getting crumbs off their table of abundance. . . . We're going to knock that table right out from under them."

The next day, Groppi, Milwaukee NAACP Youth Commandos, and Latino Brown Berets led the marchers and hundreds of student supporters up State Street. They circled the Capitol chanting "Power to the People" and stopped traffic before going inside.

"We need people to bring in food," Groppi told the crowd. "We don't intend to leave." With Latino leader Jesus Salas, Groppi led the group to the assembly chamber. Its heavy wooden doors were locked, but they yielded to the combined force of the Commandos and Brown Berets, and more than a thousand protesters flooded inside.

The Speaker of the assembly immediately adjourned the proposed special session. Most lawmakers fled the building. The demonstrators took over their desks and mounted the rostrum to give speeches about the plight of poor people in Wisconsin as the press and local sympathizers listened from the visitors' gallery. The protesters held the assembly for eleven hours, departing around midnight under pressure from law enforcement. The governor called out the National Guard to bolster local police, and for the next three weeks, the Capitol was guarded by armed personnel.

The following day, September 30, demonstrators resumed marching and chanting in the streets around the Capitol while most legislators, who had resumed their seats inside, vowed to stop any new support for welfare programs. Madison police arrested Father Groppi at a nearby Catholic church and charged him with disorderly conduct. The assembly passed a bill charging him under an obscure 1848 statute with contempt of the legislature, and Groppi was jailed for more than a month. Although the US Supreme Court later overturned their action and vindicated Groppi, the incarceration "killed his spirit," according to a fellow priest. Meanwhile, the media and public opinion turned soundly against the welfare rights movement. Though many Wisconsin residents had initially felt sympathetic, the protesters' violation of the state's most important symbol of freedom and democracy struck them as unforgivable.

During the tumultuous sixties, another activist, Lloyd Barbee, effected social change at the Capitol and helped Wisconsin catch up with the rest of the nation on civil rights. Back in 1954, the US Supreme Court had ruled that public schools must desegregate "with all deliberate speed." Milwaukee officials stubbornly resisted, and more than twenty years of legal battles were required to force the school board to obey federal law. Holding their feet to the fire was attorney Lloyd Barbee, who served in the state assembly by day and wrote NAACP legal briefs at night.

Barbee had left the Jim Crow South after World War II to enroll at the UW Law School, where racist students and professors proved that the North had its own varieties of prejudice. After graduation, he had trouble finding a law firm in Madison that would hire a black attorney. In 1961 he was appointed president of the state NAACP, an organization he had joined at age twelve in Memphis.

That same year Barbee organized a thirteen-day sit-in at the Capitol. The legislature's only black member, Isaac Coggs, was disappointed by his Democratic colleagues' rejection of bills guaranteeing fair housing and civil rights. "We have a case

of Dixiecrats," said Coggs. "The Mason-Dixon line may be just south of Wisconsin Avenue." Barbee helped bring seven hundred demonstrators to the Capitol for a round-the-clock vigil. They emulated the nonviolent tactics used at Southern lunch counters, sitting in the rotunda politely for two weeks, twenty-four hours a day, and talking to everyone who would listen. On August 14, they vacated the building peacefully after calling the state's attention to the need for reform.

Barbee moved to Milwaukee in 1962, and for the next fifteen years, he challenged the city's school segregation in the courts. Although outwardly a placid intellectual who loved classical music and philosophy, Barbee's inner passion for freedom and democracy was zealous. Friends and family recalled him often working for little or no pay and becoming "so engrossed in his work that he forgot to eat."

After being elected to the assembly in 1964, Barbee chaired or served on seven committees, worked for prison and court reform, and championed visionary causes that would not become popular

Protesters gather in the Capitol rotunda for a civil rights rally on May 13, 1961. Lloyd Barbee stands with his face turned toward the camera under the sign that reads "Democracy Not Hypocrisy."

WHI IMAGE ID 84375

A view of the assembly
chamber from the
visitors' gallery

133

Justice Shirley
Abrahamson takes
her oath in 1976.

WHI IMAGE ID 98857

for decades. During his tenure, he introduced bills in support of gay rights and decriminalization of marijuana, abortion, prostitution, and sex between consenting adults. His colleagues at the Capitol sometimes called him "the outrageous Mr. Barbee."

Finally, in 1974, Milwaukee lost its last appeal on whether its schools should be integrated. For the next two years, Barbee worked with city leaders to develop a plan for implementation. It was approved by federal courts in 1976, putting an end to the city-sponsored segregation of school children. Barbee reflected, "We are not as well off as we could be, but we are better off than we were."

In addition to civil rights, large strides in gender equality were also made in the sixties and seventies. In the years since voters chose the first three women to be "assemblymen" in 1925, more than a hundred more have followed. After Kathryn Morrison became the first woman to serve in the state senate in 1975, many women followed suit, most of them having first served in the assembly. The vast majority took their seats only after the second wave of American feminism arose during the 1970s. Since then, between twenty-five and thirty women lawmakers have represented their districts at any given moment in Wisconsin, making up roughly 20 to 25 percent of the legislature.

In 1973, Virginia Hart became the first female Cabinet member when Democratic Governor Patrick Lucey named her secretary of the Department of Regulations and Licensing. Three years later, he appointed Shirley Abrahamson to the supreme court. She was elected to the court in 1979, where she has served ever since, including tenure as its chief justice from 1996 to 2015. From 1976 until 1993, Abrahamson was the only woman on the court. But by 2016, three other women had joined her, making women the majority on the court.

Another female leader at the Capitol during those years was Milwaukee's Vel Phillips, who was elected secretary of state in 1978. She was the first African American elected to statewide office by the people of Wisconsin.

Representative Lloyd
Barbee in 1964

WHI IMAGE ID 26539

Phillips had grown up comfortably middle-class in Milwaukee's historically black neighborhood and attended Howard University. After graduating from the UW Law School in 1951 as the first African American woman to complete the LLB degree, she opened a law firm in Milwaukee with her husband and volunteered to canvas door-to-door for the League of Women Voters. Canvasing brought her into intimate contact with the city's poorest black residents, from whom she learned firsthand about poverty, overcrowding, disease, discrimination, and lack of education. "America," she said in a 1955 speech, "is not the land of opportunity it is purported to be—not while discrimination and segregation exist, and where those belonging to the Negro race can secure only second-class citizenship with definite limitations." She vowed to use her advantages for the good of the community and ran for public office.

In 1956, she was elected as the first woman and first African American to serve on the city's Common Council. For the next fifteen years, she used the position to try to end racial discrimination, especially in housing. "I was so really stunned by the conditions," she said years later, "that I just became consumed with it." Each year she introduced a fair housing ordinance and, year after year, she was the only person voting in its favor. Phillips endured blatant prejudice and sexism from her colleagues and the media, but she won the hearts of her constituents.

In 1967, she joined Father Groppi and the NAACP Youth Council to organize fair housing marches and became the target of hate mail, shouted obscenities, and violence. Despite two hundred nights of marching that drew support from national leaders, including Reverend Martin Luther King Jr., the Common Council staunchly refused to outlaw segregated housing until they were forced to by the 1968 Federal Civil Rights Act. Phillips remained on the council until 1971, when she was appointed the first African American judge in Wisconsin history. After losing the 1972 election, she continued practicing law and taught at the University of Wisconsin–Milwaukee.

In 1978, Phillips ran successfully for secretary of state, and from that office she continued her work for women's equality and civil rights. She recalled, "People would say, 'What's hardest, being the first woman or being the first black?' When I really think about it, very often there are times when they do forget that I'm a black person, but they never forget that I'm a woman." As secretary of state, Phillips was third in line to act as chief executive. Historian Genevieve McBride recalled "the time when the Governor and the Lieutenant Governor left the state and [Phillips] realized, 'I'm acting governor.' Somebody tipped off the media to do a story on it and, as she says, 'The men came rushing back, the Governor and the Lieutenant Governor, said we can't let that happen.'" Toward the end of her term, allegations surfaced that her staff had spent state time writing personal speeches for which Phillips was paid, and although she repaid the state, the controversy cost her re-election in 1983. She retired from electoral politics but has continued to be a leading figure in the state's civil rights struggles.

Milwaukee alder Vel Phillips sits in the Capitol rotunda on August 11, 1964, wearing a tag that reads "We're here for Wisconsin Human Rights Legislation."

WHI IMAGE ID 28114

The November 1978 election in which Vel Phillips made history also swept Governor Lee Dreyfus into office. Dreyfus, chancellor of the University of Wisconsin–Stevens Point at that time, was disgusted by the disconnect between legislators in Madison and the residents of Wisconsin. He was particularly mad about the state's budget surplus, saying: "I thought it was wrong for the state to accumulate that money for programs they didn't have in place and take it from the people." Though he'd never held elected office before, Dreyfus, who once called himself a "Republicrat," joined the Republican Party and launched a campaign for governor.

His opponent in the primary was the well-known Robert Kasten, who had served in the state senate before being elected to Congress in 1974. Dreyfus had almost no name recognition and little money, and he even lost the endorsement of the Republican Party. Undeterred by these setbacks, he carried out a colorful campaign, riding across the state in a school bus painted to look like a locomotive with the "Rag-Tag Band," a group of musically inclined high school students, which attracted attention wherever the insurgent candidate appeared. Dreyfus, always clad in his trademark red vest, distributed buttons and signs displaying a red vest set inside the state of Wisconsin and titled his campaign newsletter, "The Vest and the Brightest."

His eccentric campaigning style attracted media attention and, apart from a handful of half-hour television speeches, these free news stories were his only TV appearances. Dreyfus connected to voters through his sincerity and plain-spoken manners. He proved to be exactly the intelligent, unconventional candidate many voters were looking for, and after besting Kasten in the primary, he went on to defeat incumbent governor Marty Schreiber in November.

Perhaps no one was more surprised by the election results than Dreyfus himself. "Just nine short months ago the odds against this were astronomical," he told the press. "It can only happen in this nation." Asked if she was surprised, his wife Joyce replied, "I expected exactly what is happening—total chaos."

Dreyfus was unconventional as a governor, too. His closest staff shared a large office without walls, which was kept open to reporters and other members of the public. Visitors were often

Left: Lee Dreyfus flashes the victory sign as he campaigns for governor in 1978.

WHI IMAGE ID 55065

Above: Dreyfus's trademark red vest on a campaign poster

WHI IMAGE ID 97590

surprised to learn that he had no agenda and didn't want to create any new programs. Instead, Dreyfus focused on reforming Wisconsin's tax codes, reducing the cost and size of the government, and making government as transparent as possible. He also promoted good highways and a reliable oil supply, saying, "If the economy catches cold, the state gets pneumonia."

Dreyfus is also credited with giving the state capital its unofficial motto when he casually referred to Madison as "thirty square miles surrounded by reality." This was one of Dreyfus's popular sayings from the early days of his tenure, and one that he dusted off for campaigns in 1982 and 1986 in support of other Republicans. Since then, the memorable quip has been used by both detractors and proponents of the state's unique capital city, and the number of miles varies with each retelling. In fact, Dreyfus's famous phrase may have been inspired by Robert Kasten, his opponent in the Republican primary in 1978, who called Washington, DC, a "sixty square-mile cocoon surrounded by reality."

Dreyfus decided that one term was enough and chose not to seek re-election in 1982. He'd accomplished what he set out to do: revise the tax code and spend down the budget surplus.

Before leaving office, Dreyfus also signed into law a bill protecting lesbians and gay men from discrimination in employment, housing, and public accommodations. It was the nation's first law ensuring gay people the same basic civil rights as everyone else.

The idea had first emerged under the tenure of "the outrageous Mr. Barbee," who introduced a bill in 1967 to decriminalize any form of sex between consenting adults. "I think sex is essentially personal and should be treated that way," he told a reporter in 1971. "The state has no business proscribing sexual activities of parties who will consent to them." When the bill failed to pass, he tried again in 1969, 1971, and 1973, but the measure was always too radical for his colleagues under the Capitol dome. At the time, Wisconsin law regarded all homosexuals as criminals, as well as straight people who lived together "under circumstances that imply sexual intercourse" without being married.

As Barbee prepared to leave the legislature in 1976, he handed the baton off to twenty-one-year-old freshman legislator David Clarenbach. Clarenbach came from a liberal Madison family (his mother, Kathryn, helped found the National Organization for Women with Betty Friedan in 1966), had served on the city council and the Dane County Board, and was well-connected among Democrats.

With Barbee's help, Clarenbach drafted a comprehensive sexual reform bill in 1976 that would have repealed obscenity, abortion, and prostitution laws and legalized same-sex marriage. He also submitted a nondiscrimination bill that would have protected gay people from discrimination in housing. Though both were soundly rejected, like Barbee's earlier bills, they stimulated a discussion in the media about Wisconsin's archaic sex laws. The gay rights movement was gaining momentum nationwide and advocacy groups were flourishing in Milwaukee and Madison, but the culture statewide—and especially at the Capitol—lagged behind.

Representative David Clarenbach sits in the assembly chamber in 1978.

WHI IMAGE ID 67951

Clarenbach continued to introduce bills about nondiscrimination and consenting adults, meeting with stakeholders and revising the language each time to make them more palatable to mainstream legislators without undermining their purpose. Meanwhile, Milwaukee gay rights activist Leon Rouse created a coalition of religious leaders to support gay rights, including the powerful Catholic Archbishop Rembert Weakland, who endorsed the nondiscrimination bill to members of the legislature.

Clarenbach and Rouse disagreed about which approach would be more successful: a consenting adults bill or a nondiscrimination bill. Rouse persuaded his assembly representatives, Jim Moody and Dismas Becker, to back the latter, and in 1981 they worked with Clarenbach on the bill's language. Rouse marshaled the clergy—every lawmaker at the Capitol received at least one letter from a minister, priest, nun, or rabbi in their district, and clergy testified in support at public hearings—until a majority of lawmakers came to believe that ending discrimination against lesbians and gay men was the morally correct thing to do. Governor Dreyfus signed the nondiscrimination bill

Governor Lee Dreyfus signs the nondiscrimination bill into law as activist Leon Rouse (left) and State Representative David Clarenbach (right) look on.

COURTESY OF DICK WAGNER

THE WISCONSIN CAPITOL

on February 25, 1982. As with the women's rights bill of 1921, Wisconsin led the nation in protecting individual freedoms for gay and lesbian people.

Five years later, on January 5, 1987, Wisconsin's most popular and longest-serving governor moved into the Capitol. Tommy Thompson was part of a wave of conservatism that swept the nation in the 1980s and changed the state's political landscape as much as La Follette progressivism had done a century earlier. Thompson was channeling the Reagan Revolution when he cautioned at his inauguration, "Governments take freedom away from people primarily in two ways; they take away our personal freedom with too many rules and regulations, and, they take away our economic freedom with too many taxes." Thompson championed three main causes: making state government more efficient and cost-effective, creating jobs, and preserving quality of life. Although these themes immediately resonated with voters, no one would have guessed that Thompson would go on to win an unprecedented four terms in office.

Tommy Thompson was the son of a small-town grocer and a schoolteacher, and he credited his lower-middle-class upbringing with teaching him that "service to others is the greatest work of life." As soon as he got his law degree from the University of Wisconsin in 1966, he ran for state assembly, where he stayed for the next twenty years, working his way up to the post of minority leader by the early 1980s. In 1986, he decided to run for governor and reform the Capitol, which was described by one reporter that year as a place where "arrogance, favoritism and partisanship count for more than sound public policy." Backed by a sympathetic legislature, Thompson introduced a suite of conservative initiatives that aligned with Ronald Reagan's national priorities and voters' sentiments.

Welfare reform was the defining issue of Thompson's tenure, as Wisconsin grappled with how to balance compassion and fiscal responsibility. Thompson led efforts to compel welfare recipients to find jobs and to replace Wisconsin's Aid to Families with

Undated photo of Governor Thompson

WHI IMAGE ID 118697

Dependent Children program with his new program, W2. Under W2, Wisconsin's poorest residents received money for schooling and childcare with the stipulation that they would secure work within five years. The program became a model for welfare reform efforts across the nation.

Thompson also launched the first school choice program in the country, which gave low-income parents in Milwaukee the freedom to send their children to any school they chose. He also supported the state's BadgerCare program, which provided health insurance to tens of thousands of the state's most impoverished citizens. Pathways to Independence enabled disabled people to enter the workforce and keep their health benefits, and FamilyCare helped elderly and disabled citizens receive care in their homes.

Liberals criticized Thompson's W2 program for making poor families worse off, since they often had to take low-paying jobs in the service sector that didn't provide a living wage. Conservatives criticized him for not cutting government spending far enough. Yet Thompson remained extremely popular among voters and never faced a serious threat when he sought re-election in 1990, 1994, and 1998.

Thompson resigned the governorship on February 1, 2001, to accept an appointment as Secretary of Health and Human Services in the administration of President George W. Bush, a post that he held for four years. In his final state of the state address, Thompson summed up his tenure with an eye to the future, saying: "Together, we made a good life for ourselves here in Wisconsin. Be proud of it. But never be satisfied. A better way is just beyond the horizon."

At the next gubernatorial election, in November 2002, Democrat Jim Doyle defeated Thompson's successor, Republican Scott McCallum. Doyle was a dyed-in-the-wool liberal: in 1946, when he was just a baby, his parents helped revive the Wisconsin Democratic Party. After finishing college, he and his wife, Jessica, postponed their professional careers to serve in the Peace Corps. His first job after graduating from Harvard Law School was on the Navajo Indian Reservation. Like his parents, Doyle believed a strong government should help common people suffering from material, social, or economic forces beyond their control.

He began his career in politics in 1976 and won every election he entered for the next thirty years. As Wisconsin's attorney general during the 1990s, Doyle earned a reputation for being tough on criminals, including corporate offenders. For example, his six-year lawsuit against the nation's largest tobacco companies brought the state a $5.9 billion settlement. When he moved into the Capitol in 2003, many Democrats had high expectations for their party's favorite son.

As governor, Doyle focused his energy on supporting public education, expanding health insurance coverage (especially for

Governor Jim Doyle in 2004

WHI IMAGE ID 27076

children), and shifting Wisconsin industry toward biotech and renewable energy. He increased environmental protection for the Great Lakes, boosted the state's farm economy, established four-year-old kindergarten programs, and lowered crime rates and prison populations.

But his reforms were undermined by a collapsing US economy. Just as Doyle took office, the dot-com bubble burst, and the stock market plunged. Then the 2008 Wall Street crash sent the entire nation's economy into a tailspin. Stock and home values declined nearly $100,000 per household, and more than five million jobs were lost. State revenues from income and sales taxes plummeted. Without enough money to make ends meet, Doyle was forced into policies that frustrated both his opponents and his supporters.

For example, after pledging to hold the line on taxes, Doyle increased them for corporations and the wealthy. This angered conservatives, who were already upset after he vetoed bills that would permit pharmacists to deny birth control on religious grounds, require photo IDs for voting, and allow concealed carry of firearms. He infuriated liberals in his own party by making deep cuts to agency budgets, imposing furlough days on state workers, and reducing the government workforce by 10 percent. Attacked from both the right and left, Doyle responded with a single-minded passion that further alienated his adversaries. "He plays to win," wrote one Capitol reporter diplomatically.

Doyle had not run for governor in order to amputate the social programs he cherished. But every time he thought he'd cut the budget enough to deal with the latest crisis, more economic bad news would force another round of reductions. Finally, as his second term drew to a close, Doyle decided not to spend another four years dismantling his dreams of a better world. The liberal leader who'd never lost an election announced that he would not seek a third term.

The 2008 Wall Street crash that deflated Doyle's dreams ignited a grassroots conservative backlash, which the media called the Tea Party. Tea Party sympathizers had seen their homes devalued, their savings decimated, their mortgages foreclosed, and their incomes cut. They denounced liberals for spending tax dollars to bail out bankers, giving health insurance to the poor, welcoming new immigrants, and providing what they called "handouts" to people they considered "undeserving." They were predominantly working-class, rural, anti-establishment, and fed up with the status quo. In November 2010, they helped elect dozens of conservatives to the US Congress and state capitols, including Wisconsin Republican Scott Walker.

Unlike the 2010 Tea Party newcomers, Walker was a political veteran. In 1993, he'd been elected to the state assembly, and in 2002, he'd been chosen as Milwaukee's county executive. He cut the county's workforce by more than 25 percent and refused to raise property taxes. When he ran for governor in 2010, Walker's values resonated with Wisconsin voters, who sent him to the Capitol by a large margin of votes. They also enabled him to make real change by electing Republican majorities to both houses of the legislature. On February 7, 2011, Walker compared himself to Ronald Reagan as he told his new cabinet, "This is our time to change the course of history." Four days later, he ignited the state's greatest political firestorm in more than a century.

Governor Scott Walker, 2016

COURTESY OF THE OFFICE OF THE GOVERNOR

When Walker took office, Wisconsin faced a $137 million budget shortfall and state employee unions were rejecting new cuts. According to his memoir, *Unintimidated*, Walker made a proposal to his Republican colleagues: "What if we just pass a budget repair bill that gets rid of the unions and eliminates collective bargaining?" Republican leaders drew up senate and assembly bills that soon merged into Wisconsin Act 10, a law making it illegal to include health insurance, pensions, and other costly fringe benefits in public employee contracts. The bill also outlawed negotiations about workplace safety, seniority, and other labor issues traditionally defined during collective bargaining, and it streamlined administrators' power to hire and fire public workers. It allowed most public-sector unions to negotiate only modest cost-of-living raises. In Walker's words, Act 10 freed state and local government "from the stranglehold of collective bargaining rules."

Act 10 also required state employees to pay more for health insurance and pensions (this roughly equaled a 10 percent pay cut for most state workers) and halted compulsory collection of so-called fair share union dues. "Without the automatic collection of dues," Walker explained in *Unintimidated*, "the union bosses could no longer force public workers to involuntarily fill the union coffers." Walker publicly announced his plans on February 11, 2011. Republican leaders introduced their bills on February 14 and expected to move them through the legislative process quickly.

But public employees and union supporters immediately flooded the Capitol in protest. As soon as the legislation was announced, thousands of teachers, students, social workers, librarians, firefighters, police officers, and other public servants began to march outside the building all day long, every day. On February 18, so many Wisconsin teachers demonstrated in Madison that schools in several communities around the state had to close. On February 19 and 26, at least seventy thousand

Governor Walker signs Act 10 on March 11, 2011.

WISCONSIN STATE JOURNAL
PHOTO BY M.P. KING

peaceful demonstrators surrounded the building; between five and eight thousand Tea Party counter-demonstrators also gathered there on February 19. On March 9 and 10, the Capitol's upper levels were so crammed that staff worried they might collapse.

Hundreds of demonstrators moved into the Capitol with sleeping bags and occupied it around the clock for nearly three weeks. Their signs, banners, costumes, drums, and continual chanting created an atmosphere that one reporter described as "part angry protest and part carnival." Supporters around the nation paid for pizzas to be delivered to the occupiers, hallways and balconies overflowed, and the Capitol began to smell like a gym due to the constant congestion. Most of the occupiers appreciated that they were in a historic building, refraining from vandalism and even helping the custodians at times. Although officials initially thought $7.5 million would be needed to clean and repair the Capitol, the actual cost turned out to be $200,000—less than the amount spent on police overtime.

Democratic lawmakers defended the public workers and their unions, as did a handful of moderate Republicans who believed in the principle of collective bargaining. The state constitution prohibits passage of any fiscal legislation without a quorum present, so the fourteen Democratic senators abruptly left Wisconsin on February 17 and blocked the bill from coming to a vote. Republicans responded by separating strictly fiscal measures from the collective bargaining provisions and passing a new, explicitly anti-union bill that Governor Walker signed on March 11. The Democratic senators came home the next day to nearly 100,000 cheering supporters. It was a hollow celebration, however, because the power of the public sector unions had effectively been broken.

But the final curtain had not yet fallen.

Opponents of Act 10 immediately mounted a petition drive to recall the governor and his allies from office. After making their case through the media for seven months, between November 2011 and January 2012 they raised the necessary 900,000 signatures to force a recall election. It was scheduled for June 5, 2012,

and during that spring the two sides spent more than $80 million lobbying voters. When the dust settled on election day, Walker had won the governorship a second time, by an even bigger margin than in 2010, and Republicans had retained their majorities in the legislature.

Years later, as the Capitol neared its centennial, Act 10 was still being debated. In 2016, the conservative MacIver Institute announced that Wisconsin taxpayers had saved a total of $5.24 billion, two-thirds of it just by making public employees pay more toward their pensions. The institute claimed that statewide savings had amounted to about $900 per resident, or $180 per year per person. Critics charged that those savings had come at too big a sacrifice. They argued that in the wake of Act 10, expert senior staff were retiring from public service in large numbers, attracting qualified replacements for positions without union protection was difficult, and services to taxpayers were suffering as a result.

University officials argued that Act 10 and subsequent cuts had caused many faculty members to leave the state, inhibited the recruitment of new talent, and pushed UW–Madison out of the top tier of research institutions. One thing on which both sides could agree was that Act 10 had decimated the power of public-sector unions. Public sector union membership plunged from more than 63,000 in 2011 to less than 20,000 in 2016, and these unions' lobbying dollars fell by more than 80 percent.

Another indisputable consequence of 2011 was the extreme polarization of public discourse in Wisconsin as policy makers and state residents split almost evenly between Tea Party–style conservatives and traditional liberals. This division manifested at the Capitol in shouted denunciations, insults, open threats, resentment, and lines drawn in the sand. Yet, previous eras had seen equally wide ideological divisions. Pro- and anti-Vietnam lawmakers in the 1960s, McCarthy's anticommunist crusaders

Protesters outside the Capitol on March 12, 2011

WHI IMAGE ID 122071, PHOTO BY ANDY KRAUSHAAR

and their opponents in the early 1950s, Progressive Republicans and Stalwarts in 1900, and labor activists and captains of industry during the Gilded Age were all just as far apart as today's adversaries.

Even at the height of the vicious McCarthy Era, Republicans and Democrats worked amicably to solve Wisconsin's problems. Democratic governor Gaylord Nelson recalled that "fraternizing between Republicans and Democrats in those days was not seen as a treasonable offense." Speaking of his Republican opponent Melvin Laird, Nelson continued, "He would contest things vigorously, but he was always civil. He had strong convictions and great integrity, decency, compassion. We would debate all day long, and argue on the floor, and then at sundown sensibly move to the nearest pub to continue our friendly disputations into the night. It was more civilized in those days."

The Capitol's dome has always been big enough to shelter a broad spectrum of conflicting opinions. It can surely continue to accommodate a civilized sifting and winnowing of solutions to problems from both sides of every divide for many years to come.

Opposite: "Wisconsin" statue on the top of the dome before restoration

WHI IMAGE ID 44047

7

CONSERVING A TREASURE

During Tommy Thompson's fourteen years as Wisconsin's governor, he oversaw the comprehensive restoration of the Capitol, bringing the state's most important symbol of freedom and democracy back to its original glory. At the start of the twentieth century, progressive Republicans had created it as a tribute to democracy. As the century ended, conservative Republicans saved it from decades of abuse and neglect.

When construction was completed in 1917, the building's grandeur rivaled the Library of Congress, New York's Metropolitan Museum of Art, and similarly monumental spaces in dramatic effect. The Capitol was the final masterpiece of George Post, one of the country's most prominent architects, who had hired the most talented artists and craftsmen and

Opposite: This detail of the assembly room ceiling
includes a painting of an eagle and decorative plasterwork.

WHI IMAGE ID 44002

155

spared no expense in creating a lavish shrine to democracy. But his marble palace also needed to function as an office building for hundreds of state employees, and the tensions between exquisite beauty and work-a-day efficiency existed from the start.

As decades passed and the Capitol became crowded with workers, its interior spaces were carved up and rearranged. Old walls were knocked down to create new hallways, and new walls were put up to divide rooms into cubicles. Stenciled decorations and expensive hardwood trim were painted over, again and again, with whatever colors were handy. Fluorescent tubes were hung beneath stained glass skylights. Acoustic foam panels hid ornately carved ceilings. Woven Persian rugs were swapped out for cheap carpet nailed directly into marble floors. Plaster was smashed as new air-handling and electrical systems were installed. Brass railings and gratings were discarded. Most of the original furniture items—including chairs, tables, desks, and bookcases—were thrown out. Wooden window frames were replaced with aluminum. Between 1917 and 1967, thirty significant repair or remodeling projects were carried out, sometimes carefully and sometimes recklessly. Lew Porter must have rolled in his grave over at Forest Hill Cemetery.

The building had always been called "the people's house," a phrase first used in a debate in Congress in 1827 to refer to the White House ("the People's house, built and furnished by the People's Representatives, with the People's money") and applied to the Capitol during the Progressive Era. During the 1960s, as Wisconsin residents saw images of the Capitol besieged by protesters and demonstrators on television and in newspapers, they began to feel protective of the building. After it was learned that no formal dedication ceremony had been held in 1917 because the country had just entered World War I, a celebration was held on July 7, 1965, to officially dedicate it. In his remarks that day, Governor Warren Knowles called it "a living monument to the people who built our social order in Wisconsin." In the years that followed, legislators, staff, and taxpayers all began to view the Capitol not just as a workplace but also as a treasure to be honored and preserved.

Hugo Ballin's painting, "Wisconsin Surrounded by her Attributes," appears on the ceiling of the governor's conference room. It is an allegory of Wisconsin, depicted as a woman, surrounded by her attributes—beauty, strength, patriotism, labor, commerce, agriculture, and horticulture.

WHI IMAGE ID 43990

First Lady Dorothy Knowles inadvertently launched a preservation movement when she proposed painting over the dark cherry wood in the governor's conference room. She was a professional interior decorator and thought the somber, late-Victorian darkness of the room should be brightened up. But it was one of the most famous spaces in the Capitol, and her proposal sparked a discussion across state government about whether any single individual should have the power to redecorate "the people's house." The legislature responded by creating the State Capitol and Executive Residence Board to answer such questions and, although its first act was to approve her request, the foundation was laid for serious consideration of the Capitol's preservation.

Over the next decade, changes in technology sparked more piecemeal changes. After the legislature refused to fund central air-conditioning, window units began popping up all around the exterior. The arrival of personal computers prompted changes

Paint was removed from the walls of the governor's conference room to reveal the African Mahogany underneath. This is the room before renovations.

in lighting fixtures, and new electrical and telephone wires were often stapled directly into turn-of-the-century woodwork. Expanded legislative staff sizes led to more temporary walls, cubicles, and repainting. By the end of the decade, the building felt as crowded as it had back in 1928, before the first state office building had been built.

To stem the tide of amateur decorating under the dome, the Department of Administration (DOA) hired an architectural

This is the governor's conference room after renovations.

WHI IMAGE ID 45069

consultant in 1980 to draw up the official "State Capitol Restoration Guidelines." The consultant pointed out the inherent conflict in trying to simultaneously use the building as an efficient office space and maintain it as an eye-catching shrine to democracy. The report came down soundly on the side of preservation, recommending a strict limit to the number of people it could house and prohibiting a great number of specific "improvements." Legislators attacked it for "trying to turn the capitol into

An art conservator works on Edwin Blashfield's mural in the assembly chamber.

In the restored mural below, a woman representing Wisconsin is surrounded by three women representing the three bodies of water surrounding the state: Lake Michigan, Lake Superior, and the Mississippi River.

a museum" and restricting their power to hire help. Although lawmakers never formally endorsed the 1980 guidelines, the controversy raised public awareness about Capitol preservation as Dorothy Knowles had done. For example, when some Capitol workers proposed to replace the original cherry window frames with aluminum ones, the ensuing debate centered not on the proposal's cost, but on its appropriateness. Then, in 1982, the DOA spent extra money to install 150 historically accurate doorknobs around the building. The preservation trend was gaining popularity.

In 1985, a joint committee of the legislature hired consultants to address space, air-conditioning, and preservation issues. Its "Capitol Master Plan," which recommended a wholesale renovation project, was approved in 1987. Over the next decade and a half, the state would spend almost twenty times as much money restoring the Capitol as had initially been spent to build it.

The initiative began in 1988 with a pilot project to see how much the renovation would cost and how long it would take to restore the assembly chamber in the East Wing. After legislators ended their session in March, architects, painters, and scientists moved in. One major focus was conservation of Edwin Blashfield's mural, "Wisconsin: Past, Present and Future," located just above the Speaker's desk. Originally painted in 1908, the mural had been covered in varnish during the 1970s in a misguided attempt to preserve it. Its colors had become muted and continued to darken as the varnish aged. The majority of the murals in the building had suffered the same fate during the 1960s and 1970s, so finding an effective restoration method would be essential.

Conservators experimented with solvents that would remove the varnish but not damage the paint, catch fire, or injure their lungs. Once they'd invented a successful gel, they removed the old varnish from the entire 30-by-20-foot painting, one speck at a time, with cotton swabs. Chemists then sampled Blashfield's 1908 pigments on surrounding surfaces to determine the original colors and reproduced them. When all painted surfaces were restored to

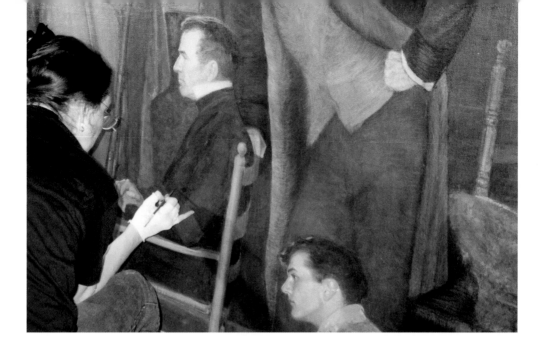

An art conservator works on "The Trial of Chief Oshkosh by Judge Doty," one of four murals by Albert Herter on the south wall of the supreme court chamber.

WISCONSIN SUPREME COURT

their proper hues, the assembly chamber had transformed from dark and dingy to bright and cheerful. And lawmakers and conservators both had a better idea of how much time and money it would take to restore the full Capitol building to its original grandeur.

It was decided that the building should be restored one wing at a time, as it was constructed, and that officials in state government would have to give up their cherished spaces for months at a time. The North Wing was chosen to be renovated first. Once the entire wing was empty—after the Legislative Reference Bureau (LRB), the Legislative Fiscal Bureau, the Legislative Council, and the GAR Memorial Hall had all moved out—technicians moved in and established a workflow that was repeated throughout the building over the next decade.

The process started with scientific measurements and photographic documentation of the existing space. Computer-generated diagrams were compared with George Post's original architectural plans, and any variations signaled places that needed closer examination. This method of comparison revealed where walls had been removed or cut into and where new walls had been erected. Both ceilings and floors were mapped, and when the two diagrams were merged in the computer, a three-dimensional model of every room could be created. Workers manually measured every doorframe, light fixture, and similar feature to populate the diagrams for comparison with the original architectural sketches. Lew Porter would have been proud.

Meanwhile, a small army of historians combed through state archives at the Wisconsin Historical Society, records preserved in the Capitol itself, and Post's own manuscripts in New York to

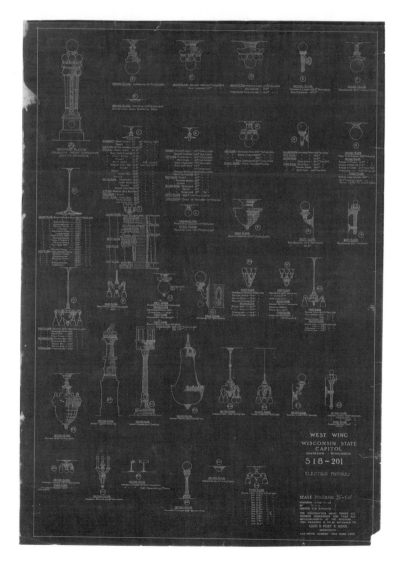

George B. Post & Sons created this blueprint of electrical fixtures for the West Wing in 1908.

GEORGE B. POST & SONS #1991/146

A conservator works on the supreme court seal.

WISCONSIN SUPREME COURT

Opposite: A conservator works with a stencil on the ceiling.

WISCONSIN SUPREME COURT

read every piece of paper generated by the original construction project. They found the names of companies that supplied interior fixtures, tracked down their advertisements or catalogs, and gathered images that showed all of the Capitol's original interior furnishings. They found contractors' manuals that explained how turn-of-the-century wiring was installed and how plaster was mixed. They inspected thousands of photographs taken by architects, builders, and tourists over the course of the previous seventy-five years to see how spaces had gradually departed from the designers' original intentions.

After analyzing all this data, renovation project leaders divided tasks into three types of work: spaces that were intact and needed to be preserved; spaces where various amounts of "improvement"

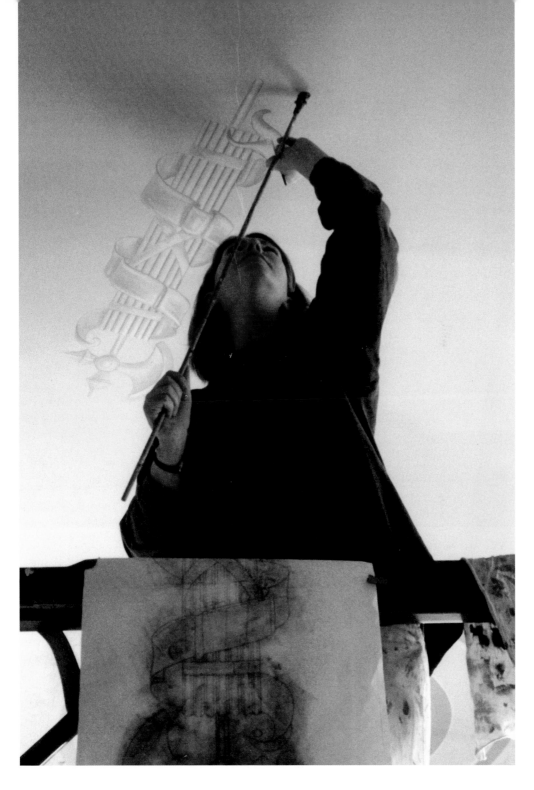

"Resources of Wisconsin" by Edwin Blashfield is painted in a segment of the inner dome that is thirty-four feet in diameter and approximately thirteen feet high.

had occurred that needed to be restored to their original state; and spaces where modern needs trumped the original plans and tasteful, harmonious renovations were required.

Executing the work was a challenge on the scale of constructing the original building. Multiple state agencies shared oversight and needed to play nicely together: the State Capitol and Executive Residence Board controlled design elements for ceremonial public spaces, occupants controlled behind-the-scenes offices, the State Building Commission controlled the money, and the Division of Facilities Management controlled day-to-day operations as Lew Porter had done between 1904 and 1917.

About 12,275 sheets of gold leaf were used to regild the "Wisconsin" statue.

WHS ARCHIVES 1991.007, BOX 2

Lawmakers, the governor, supreme court justices, and their staffs all played musical chairs during construction, moving out of their old spaces and into temporary new capitol quarters or rented offices around the Square while their wing was being treated. The North Wing closed from January 1990 to December 1992, the West Wing from February 1993 to July 1995, the South Wing from March 1996 to January 1999, the rotunda from August 1997 to October 1998, and the East Wing from July 2000 to August 2001. Some agencies, such as the LRB and the State Law Library, left the Capitol forever to take up new quarters in the Risser Justice Building across the street.

Details of the work done on plaster, woodwork, metal, and stone are described in depth in Michael Keane's essay, "Restoring the Vision: The First Century of Wisconsin's Capitol," as is the treatment of paintings, sculptures, furniture, lighting, and textiles. Readers who want an even more thorough account of the treatment of individual elements of the building, from the dome to the basement, will also find a wealth of data in the *Wisconsin State Capitol Historic Structure Report*. The full text of both documents is available online.

As layer after layer of modern additions were peeled away and workers dug into the innards of the original capitol, historical artifacts often turned up. Most of them were pieces of trash that laborers had dropped into holes long ago, the most common of which were empty whiskey and beer bottles. In some places, restoration staff discovered pieces of charred wood from the disastrous fire of February 27, 1904. Perhaps the most evocative item discovered was a handwritten note fastened behind a brass door plate in the West Wing: "This plate was put on by Fred Kinneson, Jan. 12, 1909. Findder [*sic*] please send postal." Alas, Mr. Kinneson was long-dead, but staff tracked down one of the man's descendants and took a photograph of him with the note before returning it to its original spot. They also buried their own time capsules in each wing.

In 2001, the restored capitol was designated a National Historic Landmark by the US National Park Service. Almost a century earlier, the original construction of the building had taken eleven years and cost a little less than $8 million. The 1987–2001 restoration took fourteen years and cost more than $140 million.

But it was a small price to pay for a lasting monument to freedom and democracy. As historian Michael Keane eloquently concluded, "The restoration ensures that decades from now, people will continue to make the journey to Madison, to remind themselves of their common heritage. In a hundred years, schoolchildren will still get their first lesson in citizenship under the great dome."

Sources by Chapter

CHAPTER 1

Birmingham, Robert A. *Spirits of Earth: The Effigy Mound Landscape of Madison and the Four Lakes*. Madison, Wisconsin: University of Wisconsin Press, 2010, 117.

Butterfield, Consul W. *History of Dane County, Wisconsin*. Chicago: Western Historical Society, 1880. Also contains the earliest first-person accounts of Madison.

Christiansen, George W. *Archaeological Investigations, University of Wisconsin–Madison Campus, City of Madison, Dane County, Wisconsin*. Milwaukee: Great Lakes Archaeological Research Center, June 2005; GLARC Project 04.005: 19–20.

Cravens, Stanley. "Capitols and Capitals in Early Wisconsin." Wisconsin Legislative Reference Bureau. Accessed online at http://wihist.org/2dMIYmb.

Durrie, Daniel S. *A History of Madison, the Capital of Wisconsin*. Madison: Atwood & Culver, 1874, 53–58, 65–68, 72, 82–86.

Janik, Erica. *Madison: History of a Model City*. Charleston, SC: History Press, 2010.

———. "Sacred Ground." *On Wisconsin* (Spring 2016): 24.

Smith, Alice E. *From Exploration to Statehood*. History of Wisconsin 1. Madison: State Historical Society of Wisconsin, 1973.

———. *James Duane Doty: Frontier Promoter*. Madison: State Historical Society of Wisconsin, 1954.

Strong, Moses McCure. *Territorial Legislation in Wisconsin*. Madison, 1870, 12–13.

Taylor, Hawkins. "Before and After the Territorial Organization of Iowa," *Annals of Iowa*, 1st series, 9 (January 1871): 452.

Waggoner, Linda, ed. *'Neither White Men Nor Indians': Affidavits from the Winnebago Mixed-Blood Claim Commissions, Prairie du Chien, Wisconsin, 1838–1839*. Roseville, MN: Park Genealogical Books, 2002.

CHAPTER 2

1880 Wisconsin Blue Book. "The Great Seals." Madison, 1880.

1960 Wisconsin Blue Book. Madison, 1960, 80–90.

Acton, Baron John Emerich Edward Dalberg. *Essays in Religion, Politics and Morality: Selected Writings of Lord Acton*. Edited by J. Rufus Fears. Works 3. Indianapolis: Liberty Classics, 1988, 3:519.

Britten, Emma H. *Modern American Spiritualism: A Twenty Years' Record of the Communion Between Earth and the World of Spirits*. Published by the author, 1870, 89–90.

Butterfield, Consul W. *History of Dane County, Wisconsin*. Chicago: Western Historical Society, 1880, 677.

Cravens, Stanley. "Capitals and Capitols in Early Wisconsin." Wisconsin Legislative Reference Bureau. Accessed online at http://wihist.org/2gF9jC6.

De La Ronde, John. "Personal Narrative." *Wisconsin Historical Collections* 7 (1876): 364–365.

DeKaury, Spoon. "Narrative of Spoon Decorah." *Wisconsin Historical Collections* 13 (1895): 448–462.

Dictionary of Wisconsin Biography. Madison, 1965, 118–120.

Driggs, George W. *Opening of the Mississippi: Or Two Years' Campaigning in the Southwest*. Madison: W. J. Park & Co., 1864.

Durrie, Daniel S. *A History of Madison, the Capital of Wisconsin*. Madison: Atwood & Culver, 1874, 91, 135, 139–140.

Fishel, Leslie. "Wisconsin and Negro Suffrage." *Wisconsin Magazine of History* 46, no. 3 (Spring 1963): 180–196.

Holzhueter, John. "Ezekiel Gillespie, Lost and Found." *Wisconsin Magazine of History* 60, no. 3 (Spring 1977): 177–184.

———. "Wisconsin's Flag." *Wisconsin Magazine of History* 63, no. 2 (Winter 1979–1980): 95–97.

Kutchin, Victor. "Some Personal Recollections of Governor Dewey." *Wisconsin Magazine of History* 10, no. 4, (June 1927): 411–416.

Milwaukee Daily Sentinel. "The Charter Election." April 4, 1866, Issue 79; col D.

Milwaukee Free Press. "Sole Survivor of State Constitutional Convention." April 15, 1906.

Milwaukee Journal. "When Wisconsin Had Two Governors." December 10, 1942.

"Old Abe, Wisconsin's Civil War Eagle." Wisconsin Historical Society Image Gallery Essay. Accessed online at http://wihist.org/2fNaMZA.

Quaife, Milo. "Wisconsin's Saddest Tragedy." *Wisconsin Magazine of History* 5, no. 3 (March 1922): 264–283.

Quiner Scrapbooks: Correspondence of the Wisconsin Volunteers, 1861–1865, 5: 237.

Rejected Constitution of the State of Wisconsin, 1846. Original manuscript in the Wisconsin Historical Society Archives (Series 182). Accessed online at http://wihist.org/2dLJ2Us.

Rodolf, Theodore. *Pioneering in the Wisconsin Lead Region.* Collections of the State Historical Society of Wisconsin 15. Madison: State Historical Society of Wisconsin, 1900: 378.

Smith, Alice E. *From Exploration to Statehood.* History of Wisconsin 1. Madison: State Historical Society of Wisconsin, 1973: 353–358, 653–676.

"The State Constitutions of 1846 and 1848." Accessed online at http://wihist.org/2ebV6fU.

Tallmadge, Nathaniel. Introduction and appendix to Charles Linton, *The Healing of the Nations,* 2nd ed. New York: Society for the Diffusion of Spiritual Knowledge, 1855.

Wisconsin Census Enumeration, 1895: Names of Ex-soldiers and Sailors Residing in Wisconsin, June 20, 1895. Madison: Democrat Printing Co., 1896: vi.

Wisconsin in the Civil War. Accessed online at http://wihist.org/2gtFcOW.

Wisconsin State Journal. "Pigs in State Capitol Once Made Legislature Adjourn." August 13, 1922.

CHAPTER 3

1960 Wisconsin Blue Book. "Edward Scofield, 1896–1901." Madison, 1960, 144–146.

1960 Wisconsin Blue Book. "George Wilbur Peck, 1891–1895." Madison, 1960, 136–138.

Ask the LRB. "History of the Legislative Reference Bureau" and "Chiefs of the Legislative Reference Bureau." *Legislative Reference Bureau Informational Bulletin* 88 (November 1988): 16–19.

Bradley, Ann Walsh, and Joseph A. Ranney. "A Tradition of Independence: The Wisconsin Supreme Court's First 150 Years." *Wisconsin Magazine of History* 86, no. 2 (Winter 2002–2003).

Chicago Sunday Tribune. "Legislation of Cranks. Weird Bills Introduced by Lawmakers of Oklahoma and Wisconsin." March 19, 1899: 7.

Chicago Times. "Sketch of Gov. J. M. Rusk." May 1, 1886.

Cooper, Jerry M. "The Wisconsin National Guard in the Milwaukee Riots of 1886." *Wisconsin Magazine of History* 55, no. 1 (Autumn, 1971): 31–48.

Cravens, Stanley. "Capitols and Capitals in Early Wisconsin." Wisconsin Legislative Reference Bureau. Accessed online at http://wihist.org/2gF9jC6.

Donnan, Elizabeth, and L. F. Stock, eds. "Letters: Charles McCarthy to J. Franklin Jameson," *Wisconsin Magazine of History* 33, no. 1 (September 1949): 64–86.

Fishel, Leslie H., Jr. "The Genesis of the First Wisconsin Civil Rights Act." *Wisconsin Magazine of History* 49, no. 4 (Summer 1966): 324–333.

Fond du Lac Commonwealth-Reporter. "Weekly Editor Who Became Democratic Governor Saw Many Chances to Use Humor." March 29, 1933.

Gioia, Michael. "The Accidental Librarian." *State Legislatures: The National Magazine of Policy and Politics* (January 2016): 25–27. Accessed online at http://wihist.org/2bEFyjI.

Grant, Marilyn. "One More Civil War Memoir." *Wisconsin Magazine of History* 65, no. 2 (Winter 1981–1982): 122–129.

Hanks, Lucien S. "A Footnote to the Story of a Great Court." *Wisconsin Magazine of History* 6, no. 4 (June 1923): 419–420.

Haugen, Nils Pederson. "Pioneer and Political Reminiscences." *Wisconsin Magazine of History* 11, no. 3 (March 1928): 300.

Hoke, Donald. "The Woman and the Typewriter: A Case Study in Technological Innovation and Social Change." Undated paper accessed online at http://wihist.org/2dYRFd9.

Holmes, Fred. "Judges in State Supreme Court Often Died without Money." *Wisconsin State Journal,* December 1923. Inflation rate measured at www.measuringworth.com.

———. *Side Roads: Excursions into Wisconsin's Past*. Madison: State Historical Society of Wisconsin, 1949.

La Follette, Robert M. *La Follette's Autobiography; a Personal Narrative of Political Experiences*. Madison: The Robert M. La Follette Co., 1912, 196–207, 212–218, 315.

Lenroot, Irving. "Book Notes." *Wisconsin Magazine of History* 26, no. 2 (December 1942): 219.

McCabe, Mike. "First in the Midwest: Idea to Provide Nonpartisan Legislative Service First Took Root in Wisconsin, and Then Spread across the Country." *Stateline Midwest* (March 2014). Accessed online at http://wihist.org/2bFlSgt.

Milwaukee Free Press. "Ex-Gov. Peck Is Dead." April 17, 1916.

Milwaukee Journal. "A Third of a Century of La Folletteism." October 21, 1930.

Milwaukee Journal. "The Fight that Saved Taxpayers $600,000." August 28, 1931.

Milwaukee Sentinel. "Women Employees in the State Capitol." April 1, 1900.

Smith, James Howell. "Mrs. Ben Hooper of Oshkosh." *Wisconsin Magazine of History* 46, no. 2 (Winter 1962–1963): 124–135.

Wehle, Louis B. "Charles McCarthy." *The Survey*, April 9, 1921. Accessed online at http://wihist.org/2cKP0T6.

Wisconsin Court System. "Famous Cases of the Wisconsin Supreme Court—Attorney General v. Chicago & Northwestern Railroad Company." Accessed online at https://wicourts.gov/courts/supreme/famouscases.htm.

Wisconsin State Journal. "Old Resident Has Picturesque Life: Benny Butts, Barber, Here 28 Years, Came from Dixie with Union Army." December 24, 1918.

Wisconsin State Journal. "Silencer of Dust Gave Members Lots of Sport in the Early Days of the Wisconsin Legislature." December 21, 1924.

Wright, Frank Lloyd. *Frank Lloyd Wright: An Autobiography*. New York: Duell, Sloan and Pearce, 1943, 55–56.

CHAPTER 4

Cravens, Stanley. "Capitols and Capitals in Early Wisconsin." Wisconsin Legislative Reference Bureau, 157–164.

Governor's Letterbooks. Box 178/Reel 125 (vol. 19, page 132) at the Wisconsin Historical Society Archives.

Historic Structure Report, Wisconsin State Capitol, Book I—Comprehensive Volume. Madison: State of Wisconsin, Dept. of Administration, Division of Facilities Development, 1997, 2–3, 4–16, 44–45.

Historic Structure Report, Wisconsin State Capitol, Central portion—Dome and Rotunda, Book V. Madison: State of Wisconsin, Dept. of Administration, Division of Facilities Development, 1997, 3–64.

Historic Structure Report, Wisconsin State Capitol, North Wing, Book II. Madison: State of Wisconsin, Dept. of Administration, Division of Facilities Development, 1997, 2–3.

Historic Structure Report, Wisconsin State Capitol, West Wing and Northwest Pavilion, Book III. Madison: State of Wisconsin, Dept. of Administration, Division of Facilities Development, 1997, 3–7.

Keane, Michael J. "Restoring the Vision: The First Century of Wisconsin's Capitol." *State of Wisconsin 2001–2002 Blue Book*. Madison, 2001, 113–114, 119, 126–127, 129, 139.

Kilgour, Mary. "Lew Porter, Architect." *Journal of Historic Madison, Inc.* II (1976): 32–35.

La Follette, Robert M., Sr. *Papers, 1879–1910*, Wisconsin Manuscripts QR at the Wisconsin Historical Society Archives.

Landau, Sarah B. *George B. Post, Architect: Picturesque Designer and Determined Realist*. New York: Monacelli Press, 1998.

Livermore, Joseph. Interview, 1960. Wisconsin Historical Society Archives, SC 1002.

Madison Democrat. "The Capitol Fire." March 27, 1904.

Madison, Wisconsin City Directory, 1904 and 1907.

Noll, Henry. "Henry Noll Turns Back Pages 20 Years to Scenes of State Capitol Fire." *Wisconsin State Journal*, March 2, 1924. Noll says the second death was on Memorial Day but, like Livermore, does not specify a year.

Oshkosh Northwestern. "Wisconsin's New Capitol." July 14, 1917.

Program issued by the Wisconsin State Capitol Commission, containing instructions to and information for architects submitting competitive plans, preliminary to the election of an architect for the State Capitol Building. Madison, Wisconsin: The Commission, 1906.

Sanborn Map Company, *Insurance Maps of Madison, Dane County, Wisconsin Aug. 1902*, sheet 4.

"State Capitol Spittoon." Wisconsin Historical Museum Object Feature Story, Wisconsin Historical Society. Accessed online at http://wihist.org/2c6NLjH.

Van Deusen, William A. Recollections, 1968. Wisconsin Historical Society Archives, SC 477.

"Wisconsin Capitol—Time Line." Accessed online at http://tours.wisconsin.gov/pub/Content.aspx?p=History.

Wisconsin State Journal. "Dedicate Capitol When War Ends." July 10, 1917.

Wisconsin State Journal. "One Killed, Six Escape By Miracle in Capitol Accident." October 25, 1909.

Wisconsin State Journal. "Porter Rites to Be Held Thursday." April 17, 1918.

Wisconsin State Journal. "State Capitol Burned This A.M." February 27, 1904.

CHAPTER 5

1903 Wisconsin Blue Book. Madison, 1903, 973.

Ashland Daily Press. "Another Tar and Feather Party Is Staged." April 11, 1918.

Brooklyn Jewish Center Review. "It Is Related of the Late Sol Levitan . . ." May, 1948: 10.

Brown, Charles. "The Winnebago as Builders of Wisconsin Earthworks." *Wisconsin Archaeologist* 10, no. 3 (1911): 124.

Bruce, William. *History of Milwaukee, City and County*, vol. 3. Chicago: S. J. Clarke Publishing Co., 1922, 245.

Capital Times. "18 Capitol Workers Jammed into One Room." December 19, 1928.

Capital Times. "350 Laborers Are Idle." May 1, 1939.

Capital Times. "3,000 Articles Secured During Past Year by Wisconsin Museum." December 31, 1930.

Capital Times. "Capital Workers in Cellar 'Holes.'" December 16, 1928.

Capital Times. "Capitol Employees Are Working Under Unsanitary Conditions." December 15, 1928.

Capital Times. "Capitol Girl Checks Railroads in Bathroom." December 20, 1928.

Capital Times. "Governor Becomes Winnebago Chief." August 26, 1927.

Capital Times. "Mrs. Hattie Pierce Recalls Century of Varied Activity." January 10, 1933.

Capital Times. "Office Building to House Many from Capitol." January 25, 1940.

Capital Times. "State Workers Put in Capitol 'Black Holes.'" December 18, 1928.

Capital Times. "Unsanitary Capitol Conditions Make Girls Too Ill to Work." December 17, 1928.

Cary, Lorin Lee. "The Wisconsin Loyalty Legion, 1917–1918." *Wisconsin Magazine of History* 53, no. 1 (Autumn 1969): 33–50.

Chicago Tribune. "Sol Levitan, 77, Six Times State Treasurer, Dies." February 28, 1940, 14.

Daily Cardinal. "La Mere, Winnebago Indian, Is Great Help to Museum Staff." May 15, 1929.

Evjue, William T. Review of *No Peddlers Allowed*, by Alfred Schumann. *Wisconsin Magazine of History* 32, no. 4 (June 1949): 474–475.

Fowler, Robert Booth. *Wisconsin Votes: An Electoral History*. Madison: University of Wisconsin Press, 2008, 133–146.

Friedman, Lee. Review of *No Peddlers Allowed*, by Alfred Schumann. *American Jewish Archives Journal* 4, no. 2 (1952): 101–102.

Gabriel, Mary Ellen. "Ne-rucha-ja: The Forgotten Tale of Frost's Woods and Charles E. Brown's Fight to Save It for the Ho-Chunk." *Wisconsin Magazine of History* 95, no. 1 (Autumn 2011): 45.

Glad, Paul. *The History of Wisconsin: War, a New Era, and Depression, 1914–1940*. Madison: State Historical Society of Wisconsin, 1990, 109–111, 112–116, 346–347, 390–397, 398–448.

Holter, Darryl. *Workers and Unions in Wisconsin*. Madison: State Historical Society of Wisconsin, 1999, 124–25.

Jovaag, Seth. "Sol Levitan, Wisconsin's Unlikely Politician." *Wisconsin Life*, Wisconsin Public Television blog entry posted March 2, 2016. Available online at http://wihist.org/2cjm3iA.

Kasparek, Jonathan. *Fighting Son: A Biography of Philip F. La Follette*. Madison: Wisconsin Historical Society, 2006, xv–xvi, 121–123.

Keane, Michael J. "Wisconsin Women Legislators: A Historical List." Brief 15-3, Wisconsin Legislative Reference Bureau, January 2015. Accessed online at http://wihist.org/2ejO5xn.

———. "Restoring the Vision: The First Century of Wisconsin's Capitol." *2001–2002 Wisconsin Blue Book*. Madison, 2001, 141–145, 182.

Kellogg, Louise Phelps. "The Society and the State: III. Of General Interest." *Wisconsin Magazine of History* 13, no. 1 (September 1929): 93.

Kline, Kathleen Schmitt, Ronald M. Bruch, and Frederick P. Binkowski. *People of the Sturgeon: Wisconsin's Love Affair with an Ancient Fish*. Madison: Wisconsin Historical Society Press, 2012.

La Crosse Tribune. "Oldest Settlement in State First to Report in Election." December 2, 1924.

La Crosse Tribune and Leader Press. "Sam Pierce, Messenger for Five Wisconsin Governors, Is Dead." May 15, 1936.

La Mere, Oliver. "O. L.'s Description of the Peyote Cult." *37th Annual Report of the Bureau of American Ethnology to the Secretary of the Smithsonian Institution, 1915–16.* Washington: GPO, 1923, 394–396.

Lackore, James R. *The WPA in Wisconsin.* Master's Thesis, University of Wisconsin–Madison, 1966, 28–34.

Loew, Patty. *Native People of Wisconsin.* Madison: Wisconsin Historical Society Press, 2015.

Madison Democrat. "Republican Platform." September 22, 1920.

Maroukis, Thomas C. "The Peyote Controversy and the Demise of the Society of American Indians." *Studies in American Indian Literatures* 25, no. 2 (Summer 2013): 163.

McBride, Genevieve. *Women's Wisconsin: From Native Matriarchies to the New Millennium.* Madison: Wisconsin Historical Society, 2005, 305, 307–308.

Milwaukee Journal. "St. Peter of State Capitol Has Vault to Keep His 6,000 Keys." January 7, 1923.

Milwaukee News. "106 Year Old Votes." November 1, 1920.

Milwaukee Sentinel. "German Language Barred in Grades." March 12, 1918.

Milwaukee Sentinel. "Kruegers Took Stand against Fighting in France." September 17, 1918.

Nesbit, Robert C. *Wisconsin: A History*, 2nd ed. Madison: University of Wisconsin Press, 2004, 467.

New York Times. "State Treasurer Was Once Peddler." January 16, 1927.

Putnam, Mabel R. "Equal Rights in Wisconsin." *Milwaukee Journal*, December 21, 1942.

Racine Journal. "Here Are Pictures of Oldest Women to Vote in Racine." November 4, 1920.

Racine Journal-News. "Who's Who in the Wisconsin Capitol." August 5, 1918.

Racine Journal-Times. "Woman 'Governor' Ends Term." February 15, 1956.

Ralston, J. C. "Capitol Losing Unique Figure as Sol Levitan Leaves Office." *Milwaukee Journal*, January 1, 1933.

Raymond, Tamara. "The Search for Equality in Wisconsin." *Transactions of the Wisconsin Academy of Sciences, Arts and Letters* 70 (1982): 126–134.

Salter, J. T. "Sol Levitan: A Case Study in Political Technique." *The Public Opinion Quarterly* 2, no. 2 (April 1938): 181–196.

Search, Mabel. "Women's Rights in Wisconsin." *Marquette Law Review* 6, no. 4 (1922): 164–165.

Sheboygan Press. "Samuel Pierce, Messenger at Capitol, Dies." May 15, 1936.

Sheboygan Press. "Secretary of State to Speak in City March 24." March 21, 1955.

Sheboygan Press. "State Court Can Resume Deliberations." October 19, 1932.

Smith Obituary, *Sheboygan Press*, February 21, 1968.

Tietzer, Glenne. "A Peyote Drum's Web of Significance: Oliver LaMere and Other Important Figures in the History of a Logan Museum Object." Research paper, Beloit College, 2014. Accessed online at http://wihist.org/2csofqh.

Unger, Nancy C. "The Unexpected Belle La Follette." *Wisconsin Magazine of History* 99, no. 3 (Spring 2016): 22–23.

United States Bureau of the Census. *Historical Statistics of the United States: Colonial Times to 1970.* Washington: GPO, 1975, 37.

Walsh, John Evangeline. "A Land of Extremes: Wisconsin and World War I." *Wisconsin Magazine of History* 85, no. 2 (Winter 2001–2002): 10–11.

Wausau Record Herald. "Banking House Changes Name." January 19, 1918.

Wisconsin State Journal. "$20 Million State Tax Refunds Paid." October 4, 1963: 2.

Wisconsin State Journal. "$2,000,000 in Building, Thousands of Jobs Loom for City in Works Plan." May 17, 1935.

Wisconsin State Journal. "1st Woman to Hold State Constitutional Office Dies at 95." September 26, 1991.

Wisconsin State Journal. "A Public Servant Passes." May 16, 1936.

Wisconsin State Journal. "Death Takes State Indian Guide at 60." August 12, 1930.

Wisconsin State Journal. "Dome Topples Off Statehouse." April 1, 1933.

Wisconsin State Journal. "Frank Higgins Chipper on His 90th Birthday." February 21, 1929.

Wisconsin State Journal. "Guides to Wisconsin Capitol." December 17, 1922.

Wisconsin State Journal. "Higgins to Retire on 90th Birthday." December 17, 1928.

Wisconsin State Journal. "Indian Chief Named Special Capitol Guide." May 14, 1928.

Wisconsin State Journal. "Indians Pow-Wow Tuesday to Get Old Camp Ground." October 30, 1927.

Wisconsin State Journal. "Indians Silent on Traditions Today, Chieftain Avers." March 1, 1927.

Wisconsin State Journal. "Last Civil War Vets Employed in Capitol. October 21, 1928.

Wisconsin State Journal. "Nearly All State Offices Moved." July 1, 1940

Wisconsin State Journal. "Prisoners' Hands Help Fashion State's New 'Secondary Capitol.'" July 7, 1940.

Wisconsin State Journal. "Sam Pierce, Smiling Guardian of Six Governors, Dies at 66." May 15, 1936.

Wisconsin State Journal. "The Boss Calls on Sam Pierce." May 6, 1936.

Wisconsin State Journal. "The Rambler." June 6, 1936.

Wisconsin State Journal. "The Song of the Sturgeon Is Ended but the Capitols Melody Lingers On." October 19, 1932.

Wisconsin State Journal. "Winnebago Tribe Adopts Governor." August 17, 1927.

Wisconsin State Journal. "WPA Rolls Cut; Strikers Invade Capitol, Are Finally Ejected by Police." December 31, 1936.

Wisconsin Women's Council. "Moving Wisconsin Forward: An Analysis of Wisconsin Women in Elected Office by the Wisconsin Women's Council." Madison: WWC, 2010. Accessed online at http://wihist.org/2e0tc9g.

CHAPTER 6

1950 Wisconsin Blue Book, Madison, 1950.

1970 Wisconsin Blue Book, Madison, 1970, 353–354.

1980 Wisconsin Blue Book, Madison, 1980.

Alexander, Edward P. "Chats with the Editor." *Wisconsin Magazine of History* 26, no. 3 (March 1943): 257–258.

Arneson, Eric. *Encyclopedia of U.S. Labor and Working-class History*, Vol. 1. New York: Routledge, 2007, 83.

Capital Times, "8,000 Reach Capitol in March for Peace." April 18, 1970.

Capital Times, "As War Ends, City Breathes Sigh of Relief." April 30, 1975.

Capital Times, "Nab 11 in Truax Sitdown." October 16, 1965.

Cherkasky, William B. Oral history interview with Anita Hecht, October 20, 2010. Available in the Wisconsin Historical Society's William Proxmire digital collection, accessed online at http://wihist.org/2dD3kSF, 20–21.

Cohen, Carol. "Vel Phillips: Making History in Milwaukee." *Wisconsin Magazine of History* 99, no. 2 (Winter 2015–2016): 42–53.

Drafting file, 1947 Assembly Bill 434 (microfiche from Wisconsin Legislative Reference Bureau).

Eau Claire Leader-Telegram. "Ford Stumps for Kohler." October 6, 1982.

Eisen, Marc. "The Doyle Disappointment." *WI Magazine* (Wisconsin Public Research Institute) 18, no. 3 (November 2009).

Fowler, Robert Booth. *Wisconsin Votes: An Electoral History*. Madison: University of Wisconsin Press, 2008, 157–158, 167–170.

Huffman, Thomas. *Protectors of the Land and Water: Environmentalism in Wisconsin, 1961–1968*. Chapel Hill: University of North Carolina Press, 1994, 17–21.

Index to the Journals of the Sixty-Eighth Session of the Wisconsin Legislature, 1947. Madison: 1947.

Jones, Patrick. *The Selma of the North: Civil Rights Insurgency in Milwaukee*. Cambridge: Harvard University Press, 2009, 236–239, 246–248.

Kasparek, Jonathan. *Wisconsin History Highlights*. Madison: Wisconsin Historical Society, 2004, 244–245.

Kenosha Evening News, "Pay Levels of State Employees Generally High." March 27, 1947.

Kraus, William. *Let the People Decide*. Aurora, Illinois: Caroline House Publishers, 1982.

Levin, Matthew. *Cold War University: Madison and the New Left in the Sixties*. Madison: University of Wisconsin Press, 2013, 151.

Milwaukee Journal, "When Wisconsin Had Two Governors." December 10, 1942.

Milwaukee Journal-Sentinel. "Lee Dreyfus Obituary." January 4, 2008.

National Coordinating Committee to End the War in Vietnam records, 1964–1967, Box 4, Wisconsin Historical Society Archives.

Pew Charitable Trusts. "The Impact of the September 2008 Economic Collapse." April 28, 2010. Accessed online at http://wihist.org/2hVWYuH.

Proxmire, Ellen. Oral history interview with Anita Hecht, November 18, 2008. Available in the Wisconsin Historical Society's William Proxmire digital collection, accessed online at http://wihist.org/2dDVvIR, 13–15.

Register to the Kathryn Clarenbach Papers, 1960–1989, at the Wisconsin Historical Society Archives.

Register to the Lloyd Barbee Papers, Wisconsin Historical Society Archives.

Register to the Vel Phillips Papers, 1946–2009 at the Wisconsin Historical Society Archives. Accessed online at http://wihist.org/2dX2OKo.

Rottmann, Andrea. "God Loves Them as They Are: How Religion Helped Pass Gay Rights in Wisconsin." *Wisconsin Magazine of History* 99, no. 2 (Winter 2015–2016): 2–13.

Rowley, Hazel. *Franklin and Eleanor*. Melbourne, Australia: Melbourne University Publishing, 2011, 206.

Spiccuza, Mary. "Outgoing Gov. Doyle Leaves Mixed Legacy." *Wisconsin State Journal*, December 19, 2010.

Thompson, Tommy. Inaugural address, January 5, 1987. Accessed online at http://wihist.org/2ebpLOl.

Thompson, Tommy. State of the State Address, January 31, 2001. Accessed online at http://wihist.org/2dTXeeC.

Thompson, William Fletcher. *Continuity and Change, 1940–1965*. History of Wisconsin 7. Madison: State Historical Society of Wisconsin, 1988, 425–426.

Turning Points in Wisconsin History. "Tommy Thompson and the Conservative Revolution." Accessed online at http://wihist.org/2d9mY27.

Waldherr, David P. *Dedication with Innovation: Wisconsin's Governor Lee Sherman Dreyfus*. Under-graduate thesis, University of Wisconsin–Madison, 1980.

Washington Post Book World. "Portrait of a Man Reading." April 5, 1970.

Waukesha Daily Freeman, "Joe the Monkey Visits Assembly." April 17, 1947.

WGBH Educational Foundation. "Frontline: Inside the Tobacco Deal." Accessed online at http://wihist.org/2h3FeiG.

White, Maxine Aldridge and Joseph A. Ranney. "Lloyd Barbee: Fighting Segregation Root and Branch." *Wisconsin Lawyer* 77, no. 4 (April 2004).

Wisconsin Historical Society. "Nelson, Gaylord, 1916–2005." Accessed online at http://wihist.org/2dE9oqj.

Wisconsin Public Television. "Here and Now— Gov. Jim Doyle Exit Interview."

Wisconsin Public Television. *Vel Phillips: Dream Big Dreams*. Wisconsin Public Television, 2015. Accessed online at http://video.wpt.org/video/2365403598/.

Wisconsin Radio Network. "Governor Jim Doyle on His Accomplishments in Office." Accessed online at https://www.youtube.com/watch?v=Dan6FJoJgrA.

Wisconsin State Journal covered the NAACP sit-in at the Capitol between July 31 and August 14, 1961.

Wisconsin State Journal, "Dreyfus Becomes Governor." January 4, 1979.

Wisconsin State Journal, "Hearing Turns to Monkey Business." April 17, 1947.

Wisconsin State Journal. "Kasten Expects to Run for Governor." July 7, 1977.

Wisconsin State Journal, "Our Governor Choice: Thompson on Jobs." October 31, 1986.

Wisconsin State Journal, "Picket Arrest Plot Foiled." October 17, 1965.

Wisconsin State Journal, "The Griffenhagen Report." April 2, 1947.

Wisconsin State Journal. "'The Mighty Five': Wisconsin Tops Nation in Percentage of Female Supreme Court Justices." May 8, 2016.

Wisconsin Women's Council. "Moving Wisconsin Forward: An Analysis of Wisconsin Women in Elected Office by the Wisconsin Women's Council." Madison: WWC, 2010. Accessed online at http://wihist.org/2e0tc9g.

CHAPTER 7

Google Ngram viewer search on "the people's house, Wisconsin, capitol" on October 15, 2016.

Historic Structure Report, Wisconsin State Capitol, Book I—Comprehensive Volume. Madison: State of Wisconsin, Dept. of Administration, Division of Facilities Development, 2004, 208.

Historic Structure Report, Wisconsin State Capitol, Book II—North Wing. Madison: State of Wisconsin, Dept. of Administration, Division of Facilities Development, 2003, 6–13.

Historic Structure Report, Wisconsin State Capitol. Book IV—South Wing, Southeast and Southwest Pavilions. Madison: State of Wisconsin, Dept. of Administration, Division of Facilities Development, 1995, 19–32, 64–92.

Keane, Michael J. "Restoring the Vision: The First Century of Wisconsin's Capitol." *State of Wisconsin 2001–2002 Blue Book*. Madison, 2001, 144–153, 157–186.

Rajer, Anton, and Marianne Kartheiser. "Art by the Acre: A Comprehensive Approach to the Removal of Aged Alkyd Resin on Murals at the Wisconsin State Capitol." *Post-Prints of the Paintings Specialty Group: Papers presented at the Nineteenth Annual Meeting of the American Institute for Conservation of Historic and Artistic Works*. Albuquerque, NM: AIC, 1991, 37–38.

Register of Debates in Congress. (Washington, DC: Gales & Seaton, 1829): 1372 (debate on February 23, 1827).

Acknowledgments

This book depends heavily on research done by previous writers. Three works, in particular, have proven indispensable. As the cliché says, I stand on the shoulders of giants.

Stan Cravens's seventy-two-page article "Capitols and Capitals in Early Wisconsin," which I accessed online through the Legislative Reference Bureau at http://wihist.org/2dMIYmb, maintains the high standards of thoroughness and accuracy demanded a century ago by LRB founder Charles McCarthy. Second, LRB historian Michael Keane's ninety-two-page article in the *2001–2002 Blue Book*, "Restoring the Vision: The First Century of Wisconsin's Capitol" (online at http://wihist.org/2ewQoML) brings the story up to date in similar fashion. Even a cursory glance at the citations in this book will reveal my dependence on Keane's superb work.

My third major source is almost as monumental as the Capitol itself. The six-volume *Wisconsin State Capitol Historic Structure Report*, was prepared by the state's Division of Facilities Development and East Wing Architects, LLC (Madison: 1995–2004) and is available online thanks to the University of Wisconsin at http://wihist.org/2danOAN. It's the fruit of the labor of literally dozens of researchers, historians, architects, and technical specialists who worked on the Capitol restoration from 1987 to 2001. Its roughly two thousand pages fall somewhere between a filing cabinet and a traditional book, which makes its digital edition especially important. One can only admire the tenacity, commitment, and research skills expended in ferreting out from archives and artifacts every last detail about Wisconsin's most important landmark.

Most of the color photographs included here were donated to the Wisconsin Historical Society by architect James T. Potter, along with the rights to reproduce them. Potter (1928–2014) took thousands of 4 x 5 and 35 mm photos of the Capitol throughout his life, and many of them were used in the building's official guidebook, the *Wisconsin Blue Book*, and other publications. During the 1987–2001 restoration, he captured images on almost a daily basis. We are grateful to be able to share some of his best work here.

Many of the sketches here first appeared in different form in the blog or syndicated newspaper column Odd Wisconsin, which I wrote between 2005 and 2015. Expanding and rewriting them for a new audience brought back memories of the many student assistants who helped uncover them. They dug around in newspapers and archives like archaeologists in fertile soil, and without their work few of these personal, peculiar stories about the Capitol would have come to light.

Several people deserve individual thanks. John Zimm performed detailed research and drafted sketches on short notice and in record time. Research assistants Dija Manly and Grace Castagna investigated hundreds of factual statements, correcting me when I was wrong and corroborating when I was right. Historian Rick Pifer read the entire manuscript and saved me from excessively broad generalizations and hasty mischaracterizations. Editor Elizabeth Wyckoff deftly turned my pedestrian first draft into prose that is a pleasure to read. Their generous advice and assistance greatly improved the book.

Index

Page locators in *italics* indicate photographs and illustrations.